BEFORE THE FIRES

BEFORE THE FIRES

AN ORAL HISTORY OF AFRICAN AMERICAN LIFE IN THE BRONX FROM THE 1930s TO THE 1960s

MARK NAISON AND BOB GUMBS

Empire State Editions
An imprint of Fordham University Press
New York 2016

Fordham University Press has no responsibility for the persistence or accuracy of URLs for external or third-party Internet websites referred to in this publication and does not guarantee that any content on such websites is, or will remain, accurate or appropriate.

Fordham University Press also publishes its books in a variety of electronic formats. Some content that appears in print may not be available in electronic books.

Visit us online at
www.fordhampress.com
www.empirestateeditions.com

Library of Congress Cataloging-in-Publication Data

Names: Naison, Mark, 1946– author. | Gumbs, Bob, author.
Title: Before the fires : an oral history of African American life in the Bronx from the 1930s to the 1960s / Mark Naison and Bob Gumbs.
Description: New York : Fordham University Press, 2017. | "Empire State Editions." | Includes bibliographical references.
Identifiers: LCCN 2016015548| ISBN 9780823273522 (cloth : alk. paper) | ISBN 9780823273539 (pbk. : alk. paper)
Subjects: LCSH: Bronx (New York, N.Y.)—Biography. | African Americans—New York (State)—New York—Biography. | African Americans—New York (State)—New York—Social life and customs—20th century. | Bronx (New York, N.Y.)—Social life and customs—20th century. | Bronx (New York, N.Y.)—Race relations—History—20th century. | New York (N.Y.)—Social life and customs—20th century. | New York (N.Y.)—Race relations—History—20th century. | New York (N.Y.)—Biography.
Classification: LCC F129.B7 N35 2017 | DDC 305.896/0730742750904—dc23
LC record available at https://lccn.loc.gov/2016015548

Printed in the United States of America
18   5 4 3 2
First edition

Contents

Acknowledgments

This book is truly a collective product. It stands on the shoulders of everyone who helped create the Bronx African American History Project, gain support for it in the Bronx community, and build it into a model of university–community collaboration in the reclamation of lost histories and marginalized voices.

Nevertheless, a few individuals deserve special mention. First, Dr. Peter Derrick, chief archivist of the Bronx County Historical Society, who persuaded us to start this project and who has been a steadfast supporter during the BAAHP's entire history. Second, the president of Fordham University, Father Joseph McShane SJ, and the academic deans and administrators of the university, who have given the BAAHP funding and unstinting support as soon as they realized how many Bronx residents welcomed our research and helped shape its direction.

Next, all the Bronx educators and activists who became part of our Community Research Team once they realized the potential of BAAHP to air stories they wanted told, among them my fellow author Bob Gumbs, Jesse Davidson, Nathan Dukes, Harriet McFeeters, James Pruitt, Paul Cannon, Leroi Archible, Andrea Ramsey, Joseph Orange, Jimmy Owens, and Omar Jawu.

Equally important were the faculty members, graduate assistants, research consultants, and staff at Fordham University who played an integral role in the BAAHP as interviewers, event coordinators, fundraisers, and custodians of the BAAHP's database, among them Dr. Jane Edward, Dr. Brian Purnell, Dr. Natasha Lightfoot, Dr. Oneka Labennett, Patricia

Wright, Dr. Andrew Tiedt, Dr. Noel Wolfe, Damien Strecker, Maxine Gordon, Dolores Munoz, and Dawn Russell.

And last but not least, we want to thank Fredric Nachbaur, director of Fordham University Press, for believing in this project from the minute we brought it to his attention, and Connie Rosenblum, for doing a brilliant job editing the interviews.

Preface

Bob Gumbs

Today when people think of the South Bronx, images of violence and the fires of the 1970s come to their minds. The true history of this section of the borough before this period, however, has rarely been accurately documented and told by the African Americans who lived in these communities.

Beginning in the 1930s, African Americans from Harlem, the South, and the Caribbean began to migrate to the South Bronx, then a predominantly Jewish, Italian, and Irish area. Many of these newcomers settled in the Morrisania and Hunts Point sections of the borough, living in public housing, tenements, and private homes.

I was born in Harlem in 1939. My family moved to the Morrisania section of the South Bronx in 1941 after the birth of my younger sister, Jean. My parents were from the Virgin Islands in the Caribbean. We initially lived on Union Avenue and in 1943 moved to Lyman Place, a small block of tenements and private houses between Freeman and 169th Streets.

Lyman Place was the home of two famous jazz musicians, Thelonious Monk and Elmo Hope. Leo Mitchell, who also grew up on the block, later became a drummer with the West Coast jazz trumpeter Chet Baker. Bertha Hope, the jazz pianist and the wife of Elmo Hope, lived there for a few years. A number of future artists, actors, and writers were also residents of Lyman Place.

Upon graduation from Public School 54, I went on to study music at Junior High School 40, one of the few schools in the South Bronx that had a music and art program. Some of the graduates later became professional jazz musicians and graphic artists. I attended the School of Industrial Art (now the High School of Art and Design) in Manhattan and New York City Community College in Brooklyn (now the New York City College of Technology). After serving two years in the U.S. Army, I became a graphic designer, publisher, writer, editor, and photographer.

Morrisania was home to a number of jazz clubs. In 1956, I joined the Jazz-Art Society, a group of young artists and jazz fans. We produced a series of Sunday afternoon concerts at Club 845 on Prospect Avenue. In the mid-1940s the club featured many famous jazz musicians and singers, among them Charlie Parker, Miles Davis, Dizzy Gillespie, Art Blakey, Thelonious Monk, Henry "Red" Allen, and Helen Merrill. In 1961 the name of the group was changed to the African Jazz Art Society and Studios, and we started the "Black Is Beautiful" movement, featuring the Grandassa Models, in Harlem.

In 2003, on a visit to Lyman Place, I saw Professor Hetty Fox, a community activist who has lived on the block for many years. She told me about the Bronx African American History Project at Fordham University, which was documenting the history of African Americans in the South Bronx through oral interviews of people who had lived there since the late 1930s. I immediately contacted Professor Mark Naison and made an appointment to be interviewed about my experience growing up in the area. After my interview, I contacted a number of friends about this opportunity to share their stories about life in the South Bronx.

Before the Fires tells the personal stories of seventeen men and women who lived in the South Bronx before the area's social and economic decline, which began in the late 1960s. When I reflect on my years growing up in Morrisania, I realize how fortunate many of us were to have lived in such a stimulating and culturally rich environment. I feel grateful that this book provides an opportunity to share the stories of this neighborhood with the wider world.

Introduction

Mark Naison

n the pages that follow, you will read seventeen powerful stories that may transform your understanding of Bronx history and African American life in New York. Alternately analytical and poetic but all rich in detail, they describe growing up and living in vibrant black and multiracial Bronx communities whose contours have rarely graced the pages of histories of the Bronx or black New York City.

When most New Yorkers think of black culture and neighborhood life in New York City, they think of Harlem or Bedford-Stuyvesant, Brooklyn. After reading the accounts that follow, readers will have to add the Bronx neighborhood of Morrisania to the mix. From the early 1940s through the 1960s, Morrisania was a place where black migrants from Harlem found an opportunity to raise children nurtured by strong churches, racially integrated schools, and business districts that contained some of the most vibrant music venues in all of New York City.[1]

The migration began in the early 1930s, when word began to spread among economically secure black families in Harlem that spacious apartments were available for rent in Morrisania, a neighborhood that had previously been closed to blacks. Desperate to fill their rent rolls and avoid foreclosure, landlords in that community began putting signs in their windows and advertisements in New York's black newspapers that said: "We rent to select colored families"—by which they meant families with light complexions and a securely employed wage earner. Black families who fit those criteria began renting apartments by the score in a neighborhood that offered better schools, better shopping, less crime, and cleaner air than the hypersegregated Harlem neighborhoods where they lived. And there was no violence or public protest when they moved in, in part because the community they moved into was a center of trade unionism and left-wing activism that mitigated the deep-seated racism that characterized most white neighborhoods in New York City.[2]

Thus began a period of about twenty years, long forgotten and largely excluded from histories of the Bronx or black New York, during which the Bronx served as the residence of choice for upwardly mobile black families leaving crowded Harlem neighborhoods. By the late 1940s, this once largely Jewish, working-class section of the Bronx, located on a hill hovering over one of the borough's largest industrial districts and a place that offered excellent shopping, wide streets, and good access to public transportation, had become the Bronx's largest African American neighborhood.

As thousands of residents relocated from Harlem, newly formed black churches sprang up throughout the neighborhood, once-white churches became predominantly black, and a former synagogue on Stebbins Avenue housed what would become one of New York City's largest black religious centers, Thessalonia Baptist Church. In 1951, the African American magazine *Our World* described Morrisania in terms that almost no one thinks of applying to black or Latino neighborhoods in the Bronx, past or present: "Right now, most of the Bronx's 75,000 Negroes live between 160th Street and Crotona Park South. To them, the Bronx is a borough of hope, a place of unlimited possibilities."[3]

In some respects, the settlement of Morrisania resembled the transformation of Harlem into a predominantly black neighborhood during the years before World War I. But in contrast to what took place in Harlem, where whites fled the neighborhood once blacks moved in, the movement of whites out of the community in response to black in-migration was relatively slow, giving newly arrived black residents a chance to live on far more integrated blocks and attend far more integrated schools than most Harlemites could.

In the late 1940s and early 1950s, Morris High School, located in the heart of Morrisania, was perhaps the most integrated secondary school in the United States. The experience of attending Morris was described eloquently by one of its most illustrious graduates, General Colin Powell, and reinforced in accounts by the noted civil rights historian Vincent Harding, who graduated as Morris's valedictorian in 1948.[4]

The uniqueness of this peaceful opening of a previously all-white neighborhood to black settlement cannot be underestimated. Having black residents move into a neighborhood without becoming targets of violence or prompting immediate "white flight" was not the norm in the Bronx, in New York City, or in the nation as a whole. As Beatrice Bergland's eloquent oral history in this collection indicates and *Boulevard of Dreams*, Constance Rosenblum's book on the Grand Concourse, affirms, the Jewish neighborhoods in the West Bronx adjoining the Grand Concourse were closed to black residents, except for families of superintendents, right up to the early 1960s, and police firmly escorted young black males out of those neighborhoods if they ventured there outside of school hours.

Italian and Irish neighborhoods near Fordham Road were no more hospitable. Not only were they home to few black residents, but black youth who ventured there faced grave danger from white gangs such as the Fordham Baldies. When you factor in the often violent resistance to black settlement in lower Washington Heights and the bombings and mob violence that greeted the expansion of black neighborhoods in cities like Detroit in the same period, it's easy to understand why so many black residents of Harlem were anxious to move to this portion of the Bronx once apartments became available to them.[5]

Morrisania's racial diversity, most visible in its schools and shopping districts, was not the only distinctive feature of the rapidly changing neighborhood. The community's character was also shaped by the cultural diversity of its black newcomers and by a growing Latino presence in and near the neighborhood. The first generation of blacks who moved to Morrisania from Harlem included a sizable portion of West Indians as well as people whose origins were in the American South. Hunts Point, the neighborhood southeast of Morrisania, was home to large numbers of Puerto Ricans.

At a time when air conditioning was unknown and people spent much of the spring and summer avoiding crowded apartments by sitting on stoops and fire escapes, the result was a sharing of cultural traditions ranging from food to language to music and styles of dance that existed in few neighborhoods in the nation, and perhaps the world, at that moment. On some blocks, the aroma of chitlins, curried goat, arroz con pollo, and gefilte fish wafted through the air while people could be heard shouting, cursing, reprimanding their children, and affirming love and friendship in Yiddish, Spanish, and various dialects of the African diaspora, as well as in English.[6]

But it was in music that the cultural diversity of Morrisania made its greatest and most lasting contribution. Morrisania was only a twenty-minute subway ride from Harlem and East Harlem, and the jazz and Latin music cultures of those neighborhoods moved to the Bronx along with the Harlem residents who came seeking a better life.

Some of the first generation of migrants to Morrisania from Harlem were musicians, people such as the trumpet player Henry "Red" Allen and the jazz singer Maxine Sullivan, and a love of music was deeply implanted in the lives of a majority of the residents. Once World War II sparked a recovery from the Depression, the upwardly mobile black and Latino residents of Harlem and Hunts Point became the prime audience for a profusion of clubs that opened along the neighborhood's major thoroughfares—Prospect Avenue, Boston Road, Westchester Avenue, and Southern Boulevard—some featuring Afro-Cuban music, some jazz, some rhythm and blues, some calypso.

The variety of musical forms that found a home in these neighborhoods, courtesy of street-corner singing groups, church choirs, professional musicians playing in clubs and theaters, and bands and orchestras organized in local public schools, along with the sounds emanating from record stores and apartments, made a deep impression on virtually everyone who lived there. By the 1940s, 1950s, and 1960s, Morrisania was filled with music creators and music consumers of all ages and backgrounds. As a result, the South Bronx neighborhoods of Morrisania and Hunts Point became home to a greater variety of musical forms than any community in the nation, with the possible exception of Tremé in New Orleans, as well as the residence of choice for pioneering artists in rock and roll, Latin music, and jazz.

Of these artists, some moved to the Bronx with their skills already honed, among them Herbie Hancock, Donald Byrd, Elmo Hope, Mongo Santamaria, Tito Puente, Henry "Red" Allen, and Maxine Sullivan. But others, among them the Chords, the Chantals, Jimmy Owens, Valerie and Bobby Capers, Eddie Palmieri, and Ray Barretto, learned their music in the local public schools. Cultural and racial diversity as well as great public school music programs proved to be remarkable music incubators. And all of this took place well before the rise of hip-hop in these same neighborhoods in the 1970s and 1980s.[7]

For decades, the development of the black community of Morrisania, its emergence as a middle-class suburb of Harlem, and the remarkable musical creativity it spawned were largely missing from accounts of Bronx history or African American history in New York. Scholars writing about these subjects never mentioned the two most important black churches in Morrisania, St. Augustine's Presbyterian Church and Thessalonia Baptist

Church, and music scholars passed over the neighborhood's great jazz and rhythm-and-blues clubs, Club 845 and the Blue Morocco, or the Hunts Point Palace, "The Apollo of the Bronx," whose New Year's Eve program in 1953 included Sonny Till and the Orioles, Thelonious Monk, Tito Rodriguez, and the Mighty Sparrow.[8]

Some of these omissions can be traced to the multiple tragedies that struck Morrisania and Hunts Point in the late 1960s and the 1970s. The cycle of arson and abandonment that afflicted both communities led to the destruction of more than half of each neighborhood's housing stock, and it devastated local business districts, leading to the closing of nearly all the venues that had been centers of musical vitality and cross-cultural collaboration during the two decades following World War II.

By 1980, all the small music clubs were gone, and the Hunts Point Palace had also closed, leaving local musicians without a major venue in the neighborhood where they could perform. The elected officials, foundation executives, academics, and journalists who regularly toured the neighborhood to view the devastation could see no sign of the vital music culture that had once been a source of immense local pride and creativity.[9]

Worse yet, at least for the young people remaining in the neighborhood, the music programs that had been the pride of the local public schools, and indeed the entire New York City public school system in the postwar years, were shut down entirely during the city's fiscal crisis of the mid-1970s. Schools that once had hundreds of musical instruments, which students in bands and orchestras could take home to practice with, were forced to put those instruments into storage and lay off or reassign music teachers.

As a result, musically talented youngsters whose families could not afford private instruction were deprived of the opportunity to learn how to play instruments and in the process bond with those musical artists still living in the neighborhood. While those young people ultimately invented their own form of musical expression, hip-hop, few of them were aware of the rich musical cultures that once thrived in the very neighborhood where they were now spinning records, inventing dance moves, and rocking beats.

The entire thirty-year history of Morrisania as a site of hope and optimism for upwardly mobile blacks would have disappeared entirely were it not kept alive in ritual and ceremony by those who had lived that experience. Starting in the 1970s and continuing today, former and current residents of Morrisania designated the first Sunday of every August as "Old Timers' Day." On this occasion, residents returned to Crotona Park and the small park across from the Forest Houses to barbecue, play basketball, listen to music, and reminisce with friends and former neighbors about the community they had lived in and loved.

Upward of five thousand people would attend these reunions, events that were not only unknown outside the Bronx but that somehow escaped the knowledge of scholars of Bronx history and New York City African American history. Historic memory of black Morrisania's rich social and cultural history was being preserved, but there was a gap separating those who were preserving it from those in the Bronx and the rest of New York City who were writing history, teaching history, or developing history curricula in local schools.[10]

Finally, in the winter of 2002, the gap was bridged, with consequences that would prove more significant than anyone anticipated. Dr. Peter Derrick, the chief archivist of the Bronx County Historical Society, approached me at a book party to ask if I would help start a research project on Bronx African American history because he had been deluged by community residents with requests for information on that subject, information that the society did not have.

After checking with my colleagues in Fordham University's Department of African and African American Studies, I decided to launch an oral-history project aimed at uncovering aspects of the black experience in the Bronx that were not discussed in current historical works or accessible in available documents. Starting by interviewing a small number of people I already knew, I stumbled upon a large, passionate, and knowledgeable group of people who had been waiting for years to tell stories of communities long forgotten, communities whose very histories challenged deeply entrenched stereotypes about black and Latino settlement of the Bronx.

The first of this cohort of "community historians" grew up in the Patterson Houses, a large low-income project about a mile southeast of Yankee Stadium. These people, who were friends of the social worker Victoria Archibald-Good, the first person I interviewed for the project, described the Patterson Houses in the 1950s and early 1960s as a multiracial community where people enjoyed strong camaraderie, excellent public services, and an experience of collective child rearing that helped many of them become successful later in life.

Led by a community activist and social worker named Nathan Dukes, these people arranged for more than fifteen others who grew up in the Patterson Houses, among them photographers, teachers, college professors, and professional musicians, to tell their stories, thus launching with a powerful burst of energy the Bronx African American History Project, which is what we called our research initiative.[11]

What motivated their participation was the feeling that their entire experience of growing up in a cohesive, nurturing community had been erased by media narratives that presented the black experience in the Bronx as one dominated by gangs, drugs, violence, and family decay. They said they had been trying to tell their story for thirty years but that until our oral history began welcoming their voices, no one would listen.

But even their response, which had us conducting three interviews a week by the spring of 2003, proved mild compared to what followed when the *New York Times* published an article on our research, concentrating on our interviews with Patterson residents. Within a week I was deluged with phone calls, letters, and e-mails, saying that I had started the Bronx African American History Project in the wrong place. If I really wanted to explore the black experience of the borough in depth, I had to start interviewing people in Morrisania, which by the 1940s had become known as the "Harlem of the Bronx."[12]

Two of the letters were particularly eloquent. One was from a former college professor turned child advocate and neighborhood preservationist named Hetty Fox. The other was from a graphic designer and independent publisher named Bob Gumbs. After interviewing them, I discovered that I had stumbled upon a black community whose history, when told, was about to transform profoundly our understanding of both Bronx history and African American history in New York.

I realized there were stories to be told about neighborhood and family formation, church building, cross-cultural socializing, education, economic development, musical creativity, political mobilization, confrontations with racism, and much more, stories that could occupy our researchers for years to come. Recruiting several Morrisania residents, including Bob Gumbs, as official members of our research team, we conducted over a hundred interviews with Morrisania residents over the next six years, giving us a priceless portrait of a community whose history had never made it into the written record but had much to teach us about African American and urban history in the twentieth century.

The interviews that follow are among the most eloquent and richly detailed of all the ones we collected. Two of them focus on experiences growing up in public housing, but the rest are stories that document growing up in Morrisania and adjoining neighborhoods in the years before the fires—the arson-fueled blazes that leveled entire blocks and turned much of the South Bronx into a wasteland—and thus provide a detailed portrait of that neighborhood's role as a residence of choice for upwardly mobile Harlem families as well as its ultimate transformation into a predominantly working-class black neighborhood.

With two exceptions, the interviews chosen were all with people who ended up attending college and pursuing professional occupations. There are teachers, nurses, an architect, a social worker, professional musicians, a school principal, a college professor and community organizer, a minister, a college administrator, a journalist and sports coach, a corrections officer, and a doorman, who, ironically, given his profession, is the only white person represented.

Our guide for selecting these interviews was their richness and complexity of narrative and storytelling skill. But we also made sure that we did not choose narratives that were exclusively celebratory, that overlooked the community's problems while documenting its strengths. Many of the interviews deal frankly with gang issues, drug problems, racial tensions, the wounds of poverty, the neglect of low-performing students through school tracking, and the discrimination that blacks still faced in seeking housing and employment and even moving around safely in some white Bronx neighborhoods.

Though the overall picture presented is far more upbeat and optimistic than the dominant narrative portraying black life in the Bronx, the interviewees make no attempt to romanticize their childhoods. Many of the people interviewed devoted their lives to social justice work, much of it in the Bronx, and they were determined to speak candidly about problems that public officials are often just as determined to sweep under a rug.

Equally important, the people interviewed in this book present an array of "success narratives" that few outsiders, even historians, think of when imagining black life in the Bronx. Only two of the seventeen people interviewed, James and Henry Pruitt, had college-educated parents, yet the group contains a world-class historian, a former New York City landmarks commissioner, the dean of black sports journalism, important musicians and composers, and many people who achieved distinction as educators at the university or K–12 levels. Somehow, long-neglected black neighborhoods in the Bronx and the institutions located in these neighborhoods gave these individuals the cultural capital to strive for and achieve success in occupations that were closed to their parents. How and why this happened may be the most important lessons these oral histories contain.

As you read through the accounts that follow, you will observe that people growing up in Morrisania in the 1940s and 1950s, as well as their counterparts in public housing, benefited from being exposed to an un-

usual level of racial and cultural diversity in their schools and neighborhood business districts, as well as access to strong black institutions, especially churches and extended families. This gave them confidence in their
heritage and exposure to a wider world, both of which would serve them
well in their professional lives, whether inside or outside of the Bronx.

They also benefited from schools that offered extremely strong sports
and music programs as well as from afterschool programs and night centers
that supplemented the mentoring efforts of their sometimes hard-pressed
families. Young people growing up in Morrisania or in public housing
had far more access to adult-supervised programs, whether in schools or
public parks, than their counterparts do today. The detailed account of
those programs that follows presents a challenge to policy makers and
school officials that they would do well to take seriously.

Perhaps the most remarkable feature of these interviews is the de-
scription of the incredible musical creativity this community fostered, a
creativity that crossed generational and cultural boundaries and that took
place in a remarkable array of spaces. Doo-wop singers on benches, drummers playing in the park until the wee hours, radios blasting, kids practicing their instruments in crowded apartments, the sounds of horns and
drums spilling out of music clubs, the harmonies of church choirs, and the
magic of school-hosted talent shows and dances along with multicultural
programs at the neighborhood's theaters and music halls—all these are
mentioned by people who listened to, danced to, produced or promoted a
wide variety of musical forms, sometimes to the point of becoming major
figures in the music industry. Anyone reading these accounts will come
away with a vivid image of the South Bronx as a cauldron of musical
creativity well before hip-hop arrived on the scene.

Readers, you are in for a journey, one that will take you back to a lost
era of Bronx and African American history that will excite you, inspire
you, challenge you, and hopefully make you ponder both why this experience was lost and what lessons it offers for us today. You will also meet
some amazing people who have great stories to tell.

Enjoy the ride.

Before the Fires: A Bronx Poem
Mark Naison

When I first came to Fordham
I took the El up from Manhattan
I loved the Bronx
The apartment buildings packed close together
The bars and schoolyards
The sounds of mothers calling children
Of James Brown and Tito Puente
Of stickball double dutch and dominos
The smell of hamhocks and collard greens in
my girlfriend's sister's apartment
Where hard working people cried out to God
played the numbers, and danced with abandon
While old women speaking Yiddish
remembered husbands long departed
on the streets outside
The El passed Claremont Park,
where I spent many weekends
with my girlfriend's nieces
Nobody seemed to notice that we were
Black and white
holding hands
Maybe they were just too tired to stare
Or thought we were Spanish.
I felt pride and comfort
As the El rattled on
Bringing me slowly
to my new job

—Originally published in *Bronx County
Historical Society Journal* (Spring 2004)

Avis Hanson

Avis Hanson (1924–2015) taught English at Morris and Taft High Schools in the Bronx.

My family's roots are in the Caribbean. My father was Jamaican, and my mother was Antiguan. They met in this country, and my mother was married when she was eighteen. She had come to America the year before, and she sent some of the money that she earned back to Antigua.

My father worked nights at a printing shop, and my mother worked days in the dress industry as what they called a finisher. She did buttons and buttonholes, and she was a piece worker, which meant she got paid for every dress she handled. And of course she was a member of the International Ladies' Garment Workers' Union. You had to be a member of the union; otherwise you couldn't have a job.

The owner of her shop was Jewish. His name was Mr. Block, and I remember him because he used to give my mother some lovely dresses. But most of the workers were Italian, and it was from them that my mother learned a few phrases of Italian.

I don't remember exactly where in Harlem my family was living when I was born, but when I came to consciousness at the age of three or four, we were living at 148th Street, three doors down from Seventh Avenue. This was a five-story walkup, but we were lucky. We lived on the second floor at the back, and when you looked out the window, you saw other people's backyards. But we were the poor members of the family. We had some relatives who lived up on Washington Heights, and they'd come down to visit us, particularly at Christmas time.

It was in Harlem that I got run over by a car. We were playing hide-and-seek. I was the fastest runner on the block, and I was sure I could get across the street before this car hit me, but I was wrong. They took me to Harlem Hospital to patch me up, and my father brought me flowers. It was the first time anybody had brought me flowers. I was so happy, almost weepy when I looked at them.

The way my family came to move to the Bronx was an interesting story. Every Sunday my mother used to read to me from the Sunday edition of the *Daily News*. She'd read me the funnies, and it was through her doing this that I learned how to read. One day she said to me, "You're getting too heavy to sit on my lap. You've got to read this for yourself." So I did.

Then one day in between seasons in the factory, my mother shows up in my classroom. The teacher is nowhere around. I'm sitting in the high chair. I've got the flash cards, and I'm teaching the class. I'm six years old, and I got these kids answering questions from the flashcards. My mother comes back three or four times that week and not once did she catch the teacher in the room. The teacher is down the hall having coffee with the principal.

Later I hear my mother and father talking about me and my older sister, Ivy. They're saying, "Ivy is pretty, but Avis needs an education." If you were pretty, you got married. If you weren't pretty, you'd better learn to make a buck. My mother went back to work, and there they told her that where there are Jews, there are good schools. That was the Bronx. So one Sunday the four of us put on our good clothes, went across the Harlem River, started to walk, and found P.S. 23, which was on 166th Street and Tinton Avenue.

My mother said okay, we've got the school. Now we've got to find a place where the girls can come and go by themselves. And we ended up in a walkup at 815 East 166th Street, near St. Anthony's Catholic Church.

The landlords were these two sisters, the Jacob sisters. I was amazed because I didn't think women could be landlords. But anyway, they made a deal with my parents, and my parents rented the apartment. I remember looking at the side of the building, and there's a huge sign that says, "We accept select colored tenants." I said to my father, "Are we select colored tenants?" And he says, "My child, we are select people."

We were on the second floor, and my mother got her older sister, Millie, and her husband, Josh, to live with us because we couldn't afford it by ourselves. Aunt Millie and Uncle Josh had two or three rooms, and we had two or three rooms.

When we moved to 166th Street, my sister and I had some black friends, but we also had some friends who weren't black. I can't tell you the proportion, but I can tell you one thing my teacher said it to me. "Avis, you speak so well," she said. "Who taught you to speak so well?" "I taught myself," I said. Which of course was true. Children teach themselves to speak according to what they hear.

I went home and told my mother what had happened, and she was furious. It took me years to understand why she reacted so strongly. I thought she was angry because I had the effrontery to say that I taught myself. But she was angry because the teacher had the effrontery to suggest that I had no business speaking good English.

My mother didn't have a Caribbean accent. She had a more pro-nounced New York accent than I do, except when she got mad. And my father used to correct my English. You learned at the age of four or five that you'd better match up your verbs and your subjects, even if you don't know what they are.

After my teachers got used to me, my school experience in the Bronx was positive. But you don't want to hear about my sixth-grade teacher. Her name was Miss Sullivan, and there were three things about me she did not like. She didn't like my brain, my hair, or my bosom. In those days, eleven-year-olds didn't have a bosom. She also used to feel my hair.

We used to have to wear medium-length skirts to school, but one day we were allowed to dress otherwise. I don't know where my father got this Mickey Mouse shirt, but I wore it that day. Miss Sullivan said, "Avis, when you go home for lunch today, take that shirt off. After all, there are boys in the class."

She and my mother also had this argument. Miss Sullivan wanted ten cents for lunch or something. My mother sent her a note. "For God's sake, leave her alone. I'm not giving her the ten cents."

I also remember we had an essay contest. I won everything. I won the district. We had to go to the awards ceremony on the subway. So this woman waits until I'm caught between my seat and the closet, and she says, "Avis, you have won, but you're not going to the awards ceremony because your mother can't afford ten cents for the subway."

Max, bless his heart, a round Jewish boy in brown knickers, left the boys' section, came over to the girls' section, put his hand on my shoulder, and said, "Don't worry, Avis. Being poor ain't no crime."

At the same time the teacher always had me around her desk. I would straighten it out better than anybody. I always knew where everything was. But I didn't do any extracurricular activities in elementary school. After school you came home. That's where you belong, my mother thought. I think a lot of that had to do with her panic at working and wanting to know where you were every minute.

My mother controlled my sister and me through letters that she left on the kitchen table. When we came home from school, there would be a letter telling us how late we could stay out, which vegetables to prepare for dinner, how she wanted to see the homework done when she got there. That sort of thing.

Since we were from the Caribbean, our background was Episcopalian, and we went to St. Margaret's Episcopal Church, where my brother was christened. One evening I was walking with my sister, who is light skinned, and this white lady we passed commented that "these half-caste people don't know where they belong." She objected to my sister and me because she thought we would spoil her church.

We go home, and we tell my mother. And she says, "You ain't going back there no more." So we were looking for another church.

A cousin of my father's told us about this new black minister at St. Augustine's Presbyterian Church. And my mother said, all right, we're going to try it. I remember dragging my kid brother there when he was about four and saying to the minister, this is my baby brother. That's how we met Reverend Hawkins, who became a family friend.

I was twelve or thirteen when I first set foot in the church, and I was impressed by Reverend Hawkins. I was impressed by the contrasting facets of his personality. He came across as an almost timid, shy person, but although he was gentle, he was also hard as nails.

I began to listen to him talk about the civil rights movement. One of the issues he was concerned about was what they called the Bronx slave market. Women lined up on Union Avenue at 160th Street under the El, next to the five-and-ten. The women would sit on milk crates. Whoever needed a day worker would come by, pick out somebody, and take her for a price.

I don't remember a lot of political discussion in the community or in school, people talking about the war or the Depression or any of these issues. But there were people who used to get up on little platforms. There were plenty of soapboxes. The soapbox corner was on Longwood Avenue near Prospect Avenue. And of course people lived in the street more than they do in the era of television. Television killed a lot of things. *The Ed Sullivan Show* killed the Sunday evening worship service at St. Augustine's.

And there wasn't much political discussion in my house, which is why I remained ignorant of the civil rights movement for so long. We were so busy seeing to it that the shoes were shined and there was food on the table. In those days when you had one parent working at night and the other working in the day, you had to coordinate things pretty closely.

I never saw marches or demonstrations—I only saw them in newspapers. But in the thirties and forties we saw a lot of signs of poverty and distress. We saw people's furniture on the sidewalk. That's how I learned the meaning of the word "eviction." We saw evictions routinely. But I don't think it was the sense that poverty was right around the corner that drove my parents to work so hard. I think they just grew up with the ideal that that's what you did. Nobody asked questions. You were just supposed to work.

I went to Hunter College High School. You had to take a test to get admitted, and it's still one of the hardest schools in New York City to get into.

When I was a student there, I had a job during lunch hour at a little neighborhood store on Ninety-Sixth Street, which is where the school was located at the time. One afternoon when I was late for my class, the teacher said, "Avis, it's not like you to be late." I apologized and I told her about the job. She said, "You don't have to do that any more. I'm going to get you a job in one of the offices in the school." So my name got put on a list, and I worked in the superintendent's office.

One Christmas time the doorbell rings, and there are a couple of people from the school with a Christmas food basket. My father asked me, "Do you know those girls?" "Yes, daddy," I said. "Are you going to see them when you go back to school?" he asked. "Yes," I said.

Later I went into the bedroom, and he was there crying. "What's the matter, pa?" I asked. "I let you down," he said. "When you face those girls, just keep your head up." His pride was damaged. His daughter's family had to receive a Christmas basket. He didn't realize that my name got on the list because my teacher got me into this program to work in an office at the school.

I think I always knew that one day I'd become a teacher. My mother's best friend in Antigua was a woman she called teacher Avis. And remember, I was teaching when I was six years old. I enjoy being on either side of the desk. I love the exchange of ideas.

By the time I got to Hunter College I had friends who wanted to be teachers, and I was an English major. I loved languages. I had Spanish and later French and Latin. I went to the Spanish Institute on Forty-Second Street and took a year there so at least I'd know what was going on when I walked into a classroom. My mother also let us go to the library, and the library had storytellers.

After graduating from college I worked for six months at the Veterans Administration down on Wall Street. In those days you couldn't get near a school unless you took an exam. I began in a junior high school, and that's how I wound up at Junior High School 45.

But I hadn't taken a teacher-training program at Hunter. I was an English major. I believe that if you're going to be a good teacher, you become proficient in your field.

Vincent Harding

Vincent Harding (1931–2014), a civil rights activist, a theologian, and one of America's most distinguished historians, was a friend and confidant of Dr. Martin Luther King Jr., the senior advisor to the film *Eyes on the Prize*, and the founder of the Institute of the Black World. His books include *There Is a River: The Black Struggle for Freedom in America* and *Martin Luther King: The Inconvenient Hero*.

My parents were born in Barbados and moved to the United States shortly after World War I.

My mother started out in Boston, where a brother of hers had immigrated, and then moved to Harlem in New York.

My family belonged to Victory Tabernacle Seventh-Day Christian Church on West 138th Street near Eighth Avenue. Seventh-Day Christians were a little different from the Seventh-Day Adventists, but it's an interesting difference. Seventh-Day Christians were one of the main groups of black Seventh-Day Adventists who in the Marcus Garvey and post-Garvey period became uncomfortable with the white Seventh-Day Adventist leadership. So they started organizing in Harlem and elsewhere and started independent Seventh-Day Adventist churches. But since they couldn't use the same name for their church, they came up with other names. Ours was the Seventh-Day Christian Church.

When my family, which by then consisted of me and my mother, moved to the Bronx, we never considered the possibility that such a move might mean no longer being a part of the church. The church was so central to our life that we figured we'd just get on the train and go back to Harlem to go to church every Saturday morning and Wednesdays, Friday nights, and Sundays.

The church was a combination of my extended family and my father, especially in the light of the fact that we were only two. I always felt that that church was really my family. There was a very deep sense of closeness about it. There were only about 115 members, but for me the church was a deeply grounding experience, an institution where people believed in me absolutely and expected great things from me.

From the very outset, the church provided a platform, literally and figuratively. My first public performance was singing a song there. My song was "Jesus Loves Me," and I think I was four or five. I remember that I messed up the words and ended up singing, "We are strong, but he is weak!"

In that church you went to what we called Sabbath school. You were there not simply as a sponge listening to people present information to you, but you did other things. You served as secretary of the class. You served as assistant Sabbath school teacher. You served as assistant Sabbath school superintendent. The church was very conscious of the need to develop leadership capabilities in young people.

One expectation for me was that I would eventually end up as the pastor of that church. I think I preached my first sermon there when I was fifteen or sixteen. I was at Morris High School at the time, and I still remember the text of that sermon, which was "I am the door."

There was also tremendous emphasis on culture. We had Sunday-afternoon programs called Lyceum programs where you had poetry readings, singing, quartets, piano presentations, and speeches. I also got involved with something called "dramatic reading," where you memorized poetry and memorized and delivered speeches. This was one of my specialties, dramatic reading. I started this in my early teens.

People sometimes wonder how my mother supported us, and the answer is: with a great deal of love and struggle. For most of my childhood she was a domestic, working for families downtown and in the Bronx. What was very clear to me was that she had every intention that as far as education was concerned I should go as far as I possibly could, and she'd do whatever was necessary to make that possible.

After Morris High School I went to City College, and in my last year I was in the one dormitory that City College had. When I came home I had an epiphany because I found out that in addition to her work as domestic, my mother was bringing home laundry to iron, and this was her way of contributing to whatever I needed to pay for my education. I have lived in deep gratitude to this woman.

Sometimes my mother would take me to the homes where she worked. I remember one name particularly, a Mrs. Slatin, who lived just north of Central Park. My mother must have worked for Mrs. Slatin for seven or eight years, and Mrs. Slatin was clearly interested in me and in the fact that I was trying to get an education.

My mother always worked in difficult domestic labor jobs. By the time I finished college she was working as a housekeeper at the Hotel Pierre. One of the great times in my life was when I got my first advance for my first book. I always said that I was going make a reservation for my mother at the Hotel Pierre. When we arrived, some of her friends were still working there, and they were so excited that Mabel was at the hotel as a guest.

I forgot to mention that my name comes out of my mother's work as a domestic. Around the time she was pregnant, she was working for an Italian family, and they had a son named Vincent. My mother was very impressed with Vincent. She thought he was one of the nicest boys she had ever met, and she determined that she would try out the name on her son. I got to be Vincent as the result of some very nice young Italian man, and I think that sends a powerful message.

From the time I was very young, I loved reading and learning. My mother could always find me at the library, which was on Southern Boulevard and open seven days a week. Early on I found myself loving to go to school, and I'm sure part of that had to do with the encouragement I received. It wasn't part of the culture to put somebody down because they were doing well or resent a person because they were doing well. That wasn't part of the culture at all.

I got into music when I was an adolescent. But I had a very different experience than many kids, partly because my church was closer to a kind of fundamentalist church, and so going to dance places and things like that wasn't encouraged. We did our dancing at house parties. We did our dancing when we had birthday parties or some other kind of party in people's living rooms. That's where most of our dancing got done.

We weren't encouraged go to places like the Blue Morocco, but we were encouraged to go to Town Hall. There was a preference for high culture and a sense that the blues were somehow not a part of high culture. There were more mixed feelings about calypso because calypso came out of the culture of most of the people.

Calypso was very much part of my experience growing up. My grandmother took me to events for the sons and daughters of Barbados. Just before Lent started you had all of these West Indian festivals to go to. And my grandmother danced, and my mother danced, and I danced.

When I was growing up, I thought of my neighborhood in the Bronx as something distinct from Harlem. It was clear that when we moved to the Bronx we were moving away from Harlem. In my particular case we moved shortly after somebody had burglarized our apartment in Harlem. The burglary was the major reason my mother wanted to come to the Bronx, which was considered a place where something like that was less likely to happen.

There was another difference between Harlem and the Bronx. When we lived on Dawson Street in the Bronx, neighbors knew each other, and that changed the nature of our living situation. But I have to admit that I became a member of a local gang while I was in J.H.S. 52. The gang was called the Comanche Chiefs. The young man who became the leader of the gang, what we called the captain or something like that, his name was Stokes. He never did very well in school, but he was very clear about what it meant to be a gang leader. That's what he could do, that's what he knew how to do, and that's what he enjoyed doing.

Almost as soon as I got into the gang and started moving around with them—I don't think we had got our jackets yet, but we had all kinds of plans about what we were going to get—he came on my street, on my block. All the women who were always looking out from their window or on the porch saw me with this gang, and the word very quickly got to my mother that I was hanging out with them.

My mother would not have any of it. I don't remember how long it was into my gang life, but the point came when I had to tell the gang that I couldn't be a member anymore. In those days you could get out.

I also remember that we did a lot of playing in the streets, and one of the kinds of playing was marbles on the manhole covers. There were wonderful patterns on the manhole covers [that] were great for shooting marbles. I enjoyed that a lot. Then one day I was down there playing, and somebody came up behind me and put their hand over my eyes. And I said, "Oh, shit!" and it was my mother.

When I first started thinking about high school, I was going to apply to the school of aviation technology because I'd been so involved in building models. But someone wise said to me, "That's probably not something that you want to do because that's more of a technical school than anything else."

My next goal was Stuyvesant because I knew Stuyvesant was the academic school. I had a tremendous amount invested in the idea of going to Stuyvesant, partly because of its reputation and partly because I was supposed to be a pretty bright person. But I was rejected when I took the exam, and it was clear that one of my real weaknesses was that I wasn't as good in math as I was in some other subjects.

The next place I felt I should try was Clinton. Morris High School was never even on that list, and it became an option only after Clinton said, "No, you're not in our area." Morris was kind of a last choice. And I was disappointed that I was being sent to Morris because I'd heard that the school wasn't nearly as good as these other places. But as it turned out, Morris played an absolutely crucial part in the shaping my identity and my sense of purpose in this world.

I especially remember my principal, Jacob Bernstein, and I was very glad to see his name on the wall of the school. He used to say that he wanted to make Morris a real United Nations. He used that phrase more than once. The whole idea of seeing diversity not as something you're forced into or something you're trying to avoid but as something you welcome was very important to me. I was a member of the student government, and so I got to know Bernstein and appreciate him. His vision of the possibilities of diversity was crucial to me.

For me, Morris was a kind of counterpoint to Victory Tabernacle Church. What I had at Victory and in my little family was a solid African American base from which to move. And from there I moved into a more diverse world, which was seen as a valuable thing. So the whole idea of moving from a particular cultural base into a larger society, a society into which you can bring something powerful from that base, is something we still have to learn. We have to learn how to work within American society so that you lose neither the base nor the larger multicultural society.

The most important teacher I had at Morris was a biology teacher. I never took her course, but she was my advisor, thank God. Her name was Eileen Bursler, and she really loved me. I was more than just a number on a chart of an advisee. There came a point where I knew that she cared about me. She got to know my mother, and she helped to find me summer jobs because she knew that if I wanted to go to college I was going to need those jobs.

All that was part of her role as a teacher. I don't mean as a teacher officially but as my advisor. I keep coming back to the image of her address in the upper corner of the letters that she constantly sent me even while I was in college—975 Knowlton Avenue. I used to visit her house, and sometimes she and her husband invited me to the synagogue. She was really a model teacher, one of the teachers who really marked me by her deep concern and love for me.

Another teacher I remember vividly is a woman who taught French. Her name was Helen Prevost. When I came to Morris, I had this sort of side vision of myself as maybe being an athlete of some kind because in junior high I'd been on the softball team—I think I was shortstop. But when I came to Morris, I also had an interest in journalism, and I thought I'd like to try out for the staff of the *Morris Piper*, the school newspaper.

It turned out that the tryouts for the *Piper* and the basketball team were on the same afternoon. For reasons I don't fully understand— maybe because I knew what she would say—I went to Mrs. Prevost and asked her, "Mrs. Prevost, could you help me decide what I should do about this? Both of these tryouts are on the same afternoon."

And she said to me, "Basketball you can enjoy but for a very short time. Writing, journalism; you can do that all your life." So I ended up going to the *Piper*—and being five-seven or five-eight or something like that I wasn't really suitable for basketball. Mrs. Prevost was very important to me because journalism was a path that really did open up things for me. Going into journalism represented a very important direction for a big part of my life because I've been a writer ever since.

The third teacher I remember was a biology teacher. She was the epitome of the strict disciplinarian who constantly expected that you'd do your best work. It was in my junior or senior year that I had her biology course, and toward the end of that year I had something like an 89 as a grade. I was involved in a competition with another student for the best grade-point average for the semester, and it was clear that if I had a 91 or a 92 I'd beat out the other person. I made the mistake of going to Mrs. Whatever-her-name-was and telling her that I really wanted to beat this person and could she just give me a 90?

"Vincent, I'm not going to do that," she said. "You know why? Because you're lazy." Then she said, "You could do better than that. If I encourage you, I'll be very sorry, so I'm not going to change your grade. You have to pay the consequences for not doing your best." That was a wonderful woman.

I think that my experience at Morris helped me become somebody who had a vision of a community that united people of different racial and religious backgrounds. My experience at this school was something I took with me when I created the interracial Mennonite House in Atlanta, and it helped shape me as someone who imagined a different kind of America in terms of race.

Mr. Bernstein's vision and the idea of the beloved community, a phrase that Martin King often used, were a very important part of Morris High School. When I was there, I could go through the list of students—Italian, Armenian, Puerto Rican, African American, Jewish, I'm sure there were at least a dozen ethnicities in that one place—and the principal idea was that this was something that ought to be celebrated. It wasn't just that people should get along with each other but that they should work with each other to make this a beautiful place.

I was remembering the Morris High School song, "Dear Morris High," or however it starts. I sang in the choir. The woman who conducted the choir, Mrs. Steiner, if I remember her name, was just wonderful. The choir was a multiracial choir, and one of our jobs was to sing the Morris High School song.

A lot of teachers at Morris believed in celebrating the school's diversity. It wasn't just the principal's vision. I don't remember having an African American teacher at Morris, however, and although some things were very good, even excellent, we still missed having that experience.

A few weeks ago I was involved in a pilgrimage that my friend Congressman John Lewis organizes regularly to take members of Congress to Alabama to see some of the places that were involved in the transformation of this country. Among the places we went was Birmingham, where I'd spent a good deal of time with my wife in the midst of the Birmingham movement of '63. In that period, the commissioner of public safety had been Bull Connor. But when we got to Birmingham, we began to be introduced to the Birmingham of 2005. And one of the most overwhelming experiences was to be introduced to the chief of police. The chief of police in 2005 was a black woman. That just blew me away.

Howie Evans

Howie Evans (1934–) was a sportswriter and sports editor at the *New York Amsterdam News* and a longtime basketball coach.

I was the oldest of seven—I had five brothers and one sister—and my family moved back and forth between Harlem and the Bronx because my dad was always one step ahead of the sheriff. I was born in Harlem Hospital, we moved to the Bronx when I was in the third grade, then we went back to Harlem, and came back to the Bronx in the early fifties, when I was in the sixth grade.

We lived in various cellars in the Hunts Point section because we were always the superintendents. In many parts of the Bronx, the only way a black family could get an apartment was having the father become the super of the building. We lived on Southern Boulevard, on Elder Avenue, on 167th Street, on Hoe Avenue. That particular community was probably 99 percent Jewish, with some Italian families, nine black families, and no Hispanic families.

The schools I went to were overwhelmingly white.

At P.S. 75, right off Bruckner Expressway, there were no black teachers and only nine, maybe ten black kids. Three of us lived on Bryant Avenue—at 1041, 1043, and 1045. There was a black family that lived on the opposite side of the street and two black families that lived on Elder Avenue. So we were a very small community.

The buildings were all walkups, though in our case it was a walk-down. The one time I walked up when I was helping my father clean the halls.

As for racial tension in the neighborhood—and I've seen this in all the schools I've worked at—young kids don't really see color. They see you as a nice kid. We didn't really have any problems in Hunts Point. The problem was the gang activity on the edges of the community, which eventually came into our neighborhood. A lot of the tough guys from other communities would come into the Hunts Point area. But there was very little hostility.

If there had been more black or Hispanic families, maybe there would have been more hostility. But there were so few blacks that there was no reason to have any hostility. We posed no threat to anyone— educationally, socially, or employment-wise. Because the fathers were all superintendents, we weren't taking anyone's jobs. All of my friends were integrated, but for some reason all the black guys always had their own team. We were the best athletes in that community. We had our softball team and the best Little League basketball team.

But most of the games we created and invented ourselves. There weren't many cars in the streets back then so we could play in the streets without a lot of traffic. We'd play at night; for some reason we never played in the daytime. At night we'd play a game called kick-the-can. We'd put a can on one corner of an intersection. One corner would be home plate, one corner would be first base, one corner would be second base. We'd kick the can and run the bases.

We played lots of other little games. The only organized activities we had were in the summer. Guys would come in from other communities and work in the schools. One of the guys would coach, get together a softball team.

After I was in sixth grade, we went back to Harlem. I graduated from there in eighth grade, and at that point we'd started to spend less time with our white friends. At a certain age, like fourteen and fifteen, they stopped playing with us because they started socializing with girls. That became the dividing point. They'd never invite us to their parties, and their parents would never invite us over. So we had to create our own social atmosphere.

As for predominantly black neighborhoods in the Bronx like Morrisania, there weren't any at that time, though when we moved to Prospect Avenue, that was mostly a black neighborhood. The area around Morris High School, which I eventually went to, was a black neighborhood too. As you moved closer to the school, there were a lot of private houses, and Irish families still lived in those houses. A lot of Jewish children went to Morris High School.

In those years there were music places in Morrisania like Club 845 and Sylvia's Blue Morocco, although when I was young I couldn't go to those places. Even before Sylvia's Blue Morocco there was a club on Prospect Avenue and Boston Road just as you go into Crotona Park called Kenny's. The owner was a doctor, and I went to school with his son, Howard Bowman. They were all big guys. Howard and his brother Bobby Bowman were basketball players. Bobby ended up going to Harvard University, where he played basketball. He was starting center for three or four years and was really a good player. But back then there was no avenue for blacks after college.

Kenny's had entertainment, but it was on a local scale. When they started Sylvia's Blue Morocco, they started bringing in up-and-coming entertainers. That's where I first saw the jazz singer Nancy Wilson. I was too young to get in there, but because I played basketball, a lot of people knew me, and they'd let me in. That's where I saw a lot of the early entertainers.

There was another place on Boston Road that was called the Boston Road Ballroom. It was owned by a black guy named Stanley Adams, who was one of the better basketball players at the time. He was in partnership with two friends, and they had probably the best place at that time for entertainment. All the great musicians performed there, musicians who eventually became national and international stars, like Sam and Dave, who are still performing today.

This was in the fifties, and they kept the place going well into the sixties. They got that kind of talent because they paid them better than anyone else in the city, and they paid because the crowds were there. The thing about their place was, when they said they were going to perform at nine o'clock, they performed at nine o'clock.

Some of the musicians had their best paydays playing there. Sam and Dave made their reputation there and went on to become one of the biggest record sellers in the country.

I also remember some of the jazz artists who played in the Boston Road Ballroom. There were a lot of local guys. At that time most of the jazz was in Harlem, and there were very few places in the Bronx for jazz, especially black jazz artists. Most of these jazz artists played at the clubs in Harlem, but after those places closed down for the night, some of them would come up to the Boston Road Ballroom and play there.

The place became a hangout for me. Stanley Adams was a little older than me, and we had a team called the Chryslers. He was in the Chrysler Seniors, and I was in the Chrysler Juniors. He would let me hang around because I loved music. I remember Miles Davis and Dizzy Gillespie coming up to play. And I was just amazed because these guys would sit around and talk, and then all of a sudden they'd start playing.

First we belonged to a church on Crotona Avenue across from Crotona Park—I can't remember the name. Then we became members of Thessalonia Baptist Church where I was baptized. But the church I grew up in was the one on Crotona Avenue. It was a small church, but there was so much going [on], it was unbelievable.

In a lot of African American families, if you didn't go to Sunday school, you couldn't come out and play on Sunday. So I went to Sunday school in the morning so I could come back and play. My mother would take me to church all day, and then at night at six o'clock they'd have a program for children. So I was literally in church all day until I got old enough to rebel and say I am not going to church.

I started playing organized basketball in leagues when I was about fourteen. The first time I started playing in leagues was in the community centers in the public schools. The centers became very dear to my heart because they eventually saved my life. Every public school was opened after school. They had two sessions, one from three to five and another from seven to ten. The public schools in our neighborhoods were everything to us because they were a social place, a place where we could play on an organized level. We played knock hockey, ping-pong, we had all of that. I was always in the gym.

During the early to mid-fifties, the gang activity in the South Bronx was at its peak. The gangs were highly organized, and they were huge. When I moved to Prospect Avenue, I automatically had to be in a gang. I went to a kid named Charlie Torres, who was a member of a gang that was all Puerto Rican. We were very close, and I eventually drifted into the gang with him. They called me Jackie Robinson because I could outrun everybody in the gang.

The other gangs were the Lightnings, the Penguins, the Lucky Seven, and the Slicksters, which was the biggest and deadliest gang in the

South Bronx. The gangs were highly structured and organized. They had officers, a president, a vice president, and a war counselor, who was the guy who would meet with the war counselor of the other gang and say it's time to fight. No one really challenged the Slicksters because they were older guys.

These gangs were organized around racial lines. The Slicksters were black. Most of the gangs in the South Bronx at that time were black except for the Penguins and the Lightnings. They were among the deadliest of gangs because their members had come from gang-oriented activity in Puerto Rico. So that was really a way of life to them. They were more organized than the black gangs in terms of weapons.

A lot of the guys had zip guns, which we used to make out of wood. Many of the Hispanic gangs had real guns. The gang war was so intense that there were times you couldn't go to school. If you got caught in gang activity school, you knew you'd either get killed or severely beaten.

In the North Bronx they had the Fordham Baldies and another gang that was even bigger than them. The kids in those gangs were all derivatives of their parents, many of whom were in organized crime. All along Arthur Avenue and on Fordham Road—blacks could not go there during those years. The furthest they could go was where Boston Road intersected with Southern Boulevard.

You couldn't go into Crotona Park. You could only go up to the lake in the park. If you got caught on the other side, you had some major problems getting back.

The gangs in the South Bronx would fight all the time. It was a daily thing, not once in a while or once a month. It was a way of life. Eventually, my family moved out of the gang neighborhood. We moved in with a family up on 223rd Street, along White Plains Road, near Evander Childs High School.

There was [sic] only three blacks in the school when I went there. I couldn't stay there after school because every day I had to run to the subway to get home. My first year at Evander Childs I was out of school for fifty-five days because I was scared to go to school. At the end of the year they expelled me for truancy. That's how I ended up at Morris High School. But the gangs there were just as bad. One year I missed sixty-five days because I couldn't go to school while the gangs were at war with each other.

The gangs also had all the movie theaters sectioned off. Any adults who wanted to go to the movies went downtown. The Slicksters would have one whole side of the theater and you couldn't sit there. Another group would have the middle. Every group knew exactly where they had to sit. Gangs were also in many of the community centers. You couldn't go there because the gangs said, this is our center, this is our school.

Strangely enough, despite all the gang activity a lot of the kids graduated from high school during those years. But a lot of the kids ended up in prison, and for some reason it was mostly the Hispanic kids.

There were still white kids in those neighborhoods, and they were also in gangs. The districts and boundaries were vast. The boundaries had been created well before the influx of African Americans and Hispanics in many of the schools. But the schools in the Bronx were broken down along ethnic lines, like Columbus High School, which was virtually an all-Italian school because it was in an Italian neighborhood. Roosevelt High School at one time was mostly Italian because of the Italian community. James Monroe High School was virtually an all-Jewish school. The Bronx High School of Science was for the very elite kids.

At Morris I played basketball and baseball and ran track. We didn't have a football team, but I played club football. We had a football league for high school guys that was organized by a judge named Lyons. He organized a team called the Clippers, and we played all over.

It wasn't until I was a senior in high school that people started telling me I should think about going to college. I had no idea about college. All I knew was that the college guys were playing basketball. I used to watch them play for New York University and Fordham University. NYU was the premier program, and their games were sometimes on TV.

I was playing, and in my junior year I started getting a lot of accolades. When I became a senior, I was captain of the team and made the All-City team. I got a scholarship to NYU, and I remember that in one of the first write-ups I got in the newspaper they said that I was going to NYU. At that time the school had no black players.

I would have been one of the first black players ever to play for NYU, but I never played. What happened was that Howard Can, who was the coach then, was, as I later found out, a very racist guy. One of his players had become a coach at Manhattan College up in Westchester, and he told Can about these two guys who happened to be black. My coach had graduated from Manhattan, and he had tried to get me to go there, but I didn't like Manhattan. So I went to NYU, and the two of us just dominated the other kids who were there, even some of the guys who were on the team.

Two weeks later we got letters saying that there had been a problem with the money, and they could no longer give us scholarships. This was a big problem because my parents couldn't afford college. I didn't understand any of it at that time. I was just eighteen. All I knew was a guy sent a letter saying that we didn't have any scholarships.

So I ended up going to school at Maryland Eastern Shore, which was then Maryland State. And I got there because my uncle knew the coach, and the coach was a pretty famous guy named Earl Banks. Actually, he was like the assistant coach. So the school year started, the football team was practicing, and I ended up playing football before I played basketball.

As for what got me interested in writing and becoming a sportswriter, I'll tell you something: I was horrible in English in school. You know with verbs? I was just terrible. The one teacher I remember at Morris High School more than any other was a teacher named Mrs. Ryan. I thought she was the meanest woman in the world, she was so tough. It was the only class I was in where nobody ever talked unless she asked you to talk. She was always talking about verbs and trying to show you verbs, and then she would give you assignments to write.

When I went to Maryland Eastern Shore, Congressman Adam Clayton Powell Jr. came to give the commencement speech. I was a freshman or a sophomore, and I'd never met him, but I'd seen him from a distance, and I knew that he was bigger than God in the community.

I was mesmerized by the speech he gave. I had never heard a black man talk like that, with such fury but so controlled and concise. So I went back to the dorm and wrote a story about him. I just wrote something because I was so inspired by what this guy said. Then I sent the story to the *Baltimore Sun* and they published it.

Then some guy from the paper called me and asked if I had time to be a correspondent on the eastern shore, because Baltimore is on the western shore of Maryland. So I became a *Baltimore Sun* correspondent for the eastern shore. I daresay I was probably the first black writer at that paper, although I didn't know then. But when I thought about it years later, I realized that was probably the case.

I'd write about things that were happening on the eastern shore of Maryland. I never saw the stories because the *Baltimore Sun* didn't come down that way. And I was still playing basketball and football. The writing was a once-a-week thing.

I never said to myself, I'm going to be a journalist. That was the furthest thing from my mind. I wanted to be a professional athlete, but it dawned on me that if I was going to play basketball, I had to find a way to keep from getting hurt playing football.

I played football that year, and then the second year I went out for the team, and a guy named Sherman Plunkett was also on the team. He played for the New York Jets. This guy was like 275 pounds. We called him Big Boy. He was like a monster. I'm 155 pounds. This guy comes out, I'm running around the end and nobody's blocking him. I see this guy coming at me, and I stop cold in my tracks. I said, "Big Boy, please don't hit me." He's getting ready to put the wood on me. Two days later I told the coach, I'm done.

As for basketball, in those days it was pretty hard to make the NBA from a black college. When I was in Maryland, all the greatest black athletes in the United States were in black schools, but none of the white schools would play them. The coaches would never schedule games with them because they couldn't compete with the black players. Most of the schools in the Atlantic Coast Conference took everything from the black coaches. The Harlem Globetrotters did the highest recruiting of black players.

When I graduated, I came back to New York. A guy named Jack Bernstein, who was the supervisor of a school district in the Bronx, assigned me to the community center at P.S. 99. I had a lot of history at that center. In my teens, when I was living on Prospect Avenue, P.S. 99 was on Stebbins Avenue, a block away from where I lived, and it became a safe haven for me because my parents would let me travel that far.

At P.S. 99, one of the people there who saved my life was a guy named Vincent Tibbs. I'll tell you what happened. I was the president of the Youth Council, and we used to give affairs. One night we were having a dance contest. There was a newly organized gang that had come from Boston Road. They all wore black silk shirts and pants, and they were all big guys. Everybody was like, "Who are these guys? Where'd they come from?"

They didn't have a name, but they'd just come in and create havoc. Everybody was intimidated by them. I was trying to clear the floor so we could have a mambo contest. Now, to set the stage for what happened, you need to know that the day before, my father hit the number for about six thousand dollars. He bought me two suits. I remember I went down to Delancey Street to get them. One was a tan double-breasted suit. I wasn't supposed to be wearing this suit before Easter Sunday.

So I put this suit on because we're having the dance on Friday. I'm trying to clear the floor. These guys stood in the middle of the floor. I said, "You got to get off the floor, man, we trying to have this contest." One guy pulls out a knife, swings at me, and cuts the inside of my jacket. If my jacket hadn't been open, I probably would have gotten slashed.

Everybody went crazy and ran out. I'm going out after them, and Mr. Tibbs comes and grabs me and takes me in his office. I'm furious, and all my boys are outside waiting. This guy Mr. Tibbs stands in front of the door, and he starts telling me, "You have a chance to do something with your life."

"You're one of the best athletes in the neighborhood," he said. "And you gonna go out in the street and get killed over this. Howie, the only way you are going to get through that door is you got to come through me."

He stood in front of the door, and I'm crying, tears are coming down my face. But he would not let me out that door until the whole street was cleared. I wasn't afraid of those guys. The only thing I was afraid of was to go home and tell my father my suit was cut up.

All the time I was in college I worked in community centers. I got a Board of Education license and was probably the only person who ever got one before going to college. There was this Jewish guy who was a wheeler-dealer. He was really impressed by my leadership, by the way I could control people and how they gravitated toward me. He thought that the guys in the gangs would listen to me and respect me. So he got me a Board of Education license, no. 180255. For the next thirty years that was my number.

This let me be a teacher in the community centers.

Before college I'd worked in the summer playgrounds, and eventually I got a Board of Education license to teach, but they didn't change my file number. They paid you by a file number, and throughout my career in education, that number never changed.

When I came back from college, I didn't go directly into teaching. I started working in the Board of Education's afterschool program in community centers, and later on I started teaching at a junior high school. This was in Sunnyside, Queens. They wanted a black guy because there were no black teachers.

I'd never really been to Queens. So I went out there to meet the principal, a Dutchman. I said, look, I already got the job, but I'd like to make a deal with you. Nobody wanted to do yard and lunch duty.

That was around the time they started busing in black kids. They were busing black kids from Jamaica into Sunnyside, which was an Irish and Italian community. Basically they were looking for a tough guy, somebody who could control these kids, whom they thought were bad. I told him, these kids aren't going be tougher than me.

So the first day I get into the school, I see this big huge kid walking through. I was teaching a gym class. I was a sub, and if any black teacher didn't show up I would sub in those classes. I see this big guy walking to the school, so I asked him, "Where's the gym?" He says, "I don't know." I looked at this guy and said, "What do you mean you don't know? Don't you play basketball?" He said no. So I get down to the gym and I'm talking with another teacher who's the basketball coach.

I said, "I saw a big kid walking in the halls who told me he don't play basketball." "Oh, that's Lenny Elmore," the coach said. And I asked, "What do you mean he doesn't play?" "He can't play," the coach said. I said, "Why don't you teach him to play? He's the biggest kid in the school. He looks like thirteen years old and he's six-six." The coach didn't want to teach him. So I said, "Well, I'll teach this guy how to play." I went and got the kid and said, "Look, are you interested in learning how to play basketball?" He said, "Yes, but you've got to ask my mother."

So we get in the car, and I drive him to his home in Queens. His father works for the sanitation department; his mother was a nurse. His mother says, "Mr. Evans, Lenny has asthma. That is why we don't let him play basketball." I said, "Mrs. Elmore, at his age, through exercise he can overcome asthma. Just give me the opportunity."

I take Lenny out, and we started playing. Then I said, "Are you interested in going to a high school?" I went to talk to his parents and I said, "I've got some friends over at Power Memorial, and I think I can get him in." Note, this kid has never played a full-court game of basketball in his life. So I load up five kids. One kid was a baseball player, an Irish kid who was a very good athlete. He was better than the other kids who played baseball and basketball.

I take them over to Power Memorial, and the coach puts them in a full-court game. They start playing, and all of a sudden this kid Elmore is blocking shots, bam bam bam. I am like amazed he hasn't ever played. All I did was place him underneath the basket doing drills and stuff. That is how he got into Power and eventually became an All-City player. He was smart, and he worked hard. He got a scholarship to Maryland.

The way I met Hilton White, the famous basketball coach and mentor to so many kids who grew up in Morrisania, was like this. Hilton had two jobs, like all of us did then. He worked for the Parks Department, and then at night he worked in the community centers. Hilton took the basketball team to a higher level because he didn't have to run the center; he just had to run the basketball team. Hilton was working I think at P.S. 120, on Caldwell Avenue, and I was at P.S. 60, on Stebbins Avenue, off Westchester Avenue and Dawson Street. These were the dominant programs in the Bronx.

This was a time when New York City had the best basketball in the country, and I think the community centers were very much responsible for producing so many great players. The centers were the dominant factor, just like the Amateur Athletic Union programs are now. We became the dominant people in the kids' lives because the coaches would see them from October to Christmas time, but after Christmas the season was over unless you went to the playoffs. So we had the kids in the community centers for nine months of the year.

The recruiting was different back then. The college coaches knew that the community center people were the key. Coaches would come to the schools and the playgrounds. They didn't have all of the restrictions they have now. At Christmas, the high school coaches all wanted to get out of school and go up to the mountains, and when June 30 came, they were the first ones out of the building.

I was very involved in the Rucker Tournament. I refereed and coached in it. I also played in the tournament. Holcombe Rucker and I were very close. I was working in the Bronx at P.S. 60, and he was working out at St. Phillips in Harlem. Once a week he'd bring up five teams to play at P.S. 60 because we had a gym and he didn't have one available. So he'd bring his kids up to the Bronx to play, and we'd play all night. When Rucker died in 1965, we formed the Holcombe Rucker Memorial Committee. The goal was to keep the Rucker Tournament and the Rucker League in Harlem.

The way I started covering sports for the *Amsterdam News* in New York was like this. I was very friendly with Wilt Chamberlain, who used to come to New York all the time. We used to play at Mount Morris Park.

He'd just drive up, and we'd play. At that time they were dogging him in the newspapers and magazines and writing all these horrible stories about him. I was infuriated. I was considered a militant at that point. So I said, I'm going to write a story in reaction to what all these magazine people were writing about him. I took it down to the *Amsterdam News,* and they published it. When the story came out, it got such a great reaction that a week later the editor of the paper called me and asked if I wanted to contribute a story to the paper every week. That's how I started.

Then I became a weekly columnist and a writer. In 1965 I started covering the New York Jets. I was the only black sportswriter covering professional football. And I've been writing ever since.

Henry Pruitt

Henry Pruitt (1934–) has been an educator, a professor, and a writer.

One of my first memories of growing up in the Bronx is of Crotona Park, which had a pond and still does. That pond was interesting because it was stocked with sunfish, catfish, and crawfish. One day when I was in elementary school my buddy Albert Abdul and I did very well in catching crawfish. We caught maybe forty or fifty of them. We brought them home to put in the fish tank and kind of observe them. But before we could do that, Mrs. Abdul saw the bucket of crawfish and put them in a pot. So we ended up having crawfish that afternoon for a snack.

My father didn't care much for fishing, but I went to Camp Minisink, in Port Jervis, north of the city, which had a catfish pond. And there I had a fishing counselor named Pop Nevilles, who was from New York and who taught me how to fish. I was one of his most outstanding students, so in the fall, after camp was over, he took me fishing in the city. He was the first person who put a rod and reel in my hands.

When somebody teaches you to fish, they tell you that you have to be patient. They tell you that you have to have the correct bait, and you have to be in the right place at the right time, because you can be in the same place at different times and one time catch no fish and another time catch a lot of fish.

Pop Nevilles also taught us that part of fishing was cleaning the fish. We used to have fish frys at Minisink. We'd catch a bunch of catfish and clean them up and have them for dinner. In a two-week period we might have catfish frys once or twice.

Pop Nevilles lived on Undercliff Avenue, along the Harlem River in the West Bronx. When he took me fishing in New York, we'd fish off the piers in the Hudson River and catch something called tommy cod. You catch them with sandworms. Tommy cods were less than twelve inches long, absolutely delicious, and they'd come in the winter.

I'm not sure how I started fishing in the Bronx River, but the Bronx River in my history is four different places. The first place was West Farms, and at West Farms there's a falls that goes into the river and comes out into Upper New York Bay. And crabs would come into the falls, carp would come into the falls, and we could sit in West Farms and catch carp and catch crabs. I'm not sure if we were supposed to eat them.

Also at West Farms you'd see the eels come into the river in the springtime. The eels were two or three inches long, shaped like regular eels, and they'd go up the river. And if you went north of West Farms, inside Bronx Park, there's a very big falls, and at the base of that falls you'd catch carp and white perch. And you'd see the eels climbing up the wall of the falls to go into the upper river. You could actually see them.

Mostly I fished by myself. I'd get on the bus, get to where Bronx Park starts, and I could fish at West Farms. A little farther north, you could fish on the other side of Bronx Park from the zoo. You could just climb down and fish up to the main falls.

They discouraged you from fishing in the main Bronx Park Zoo, but at Fordham Road the Bronx River went underneath the highway. And you could climb down under the highway, and there was a place where you could get access to the river and fish for carp, right at Fordham Road at the entrance to Bronx Park. Then you could go further north to the Bronx River Parkway where it becomes that very curvaceous road up in the Yonkers area.

The fish of merit there was goldfish, not carp. You'd look in the water and you'd see hundreds of goldfish, and we'd catch the goldfish, take them home, and put them in the tank. Goldfish came in all flavors. There were black ones, brown ones, gold ones, spotted ones, white ones. We got a big kick out of catching goldfish, so we fished there.

Also in that area, north of the Bronx county line in Westchester, there's another river called the Saw Mill River. The Saw Mill River was loaded with carp. I've eaten carp, but you only need to do that once. That's if you don't know how to fix them, because carp tastes like mud. But catching carp is really thrilling because they're very strong. I've lost two or three rods trying to catch carp. Carp get to be ten or fifteen or twenty pounds. So if you put your line down on the ground and talk to your neighbor, you may see your line going across the lake because the fish will snatch it.

As I was growing up in the Bronx, I'd find different spots to fish. The Bronx River was one site; that was for freshwater fish. Then we'd fish on Orchard Beach. At Orchard Beach you'd catch flounders, and you'd catch striped bass casting from the jetties. And there's a place called the lagoon on the back end of Orchard Beach near a parking lot, and you could catch flounders there in the winter. So we would fish there. When I was young I'd climb out on the jetties in Orchard Beach and fish, but I cut that out recently.

I used to see other people fishing at these kinds of obscure places, but the camaraderie among them came later. I have a place now called the Englewood Boat Basin on the Hudson River, and there are people who fish there every day. So you come down there, and you see the same guys you saw the day before. I'd only go maybe once a week or so. But there are people who camp there, put up their pup tents. They're there every single day. They fish year round, except when it's unbelievably cold. And the fishing in the Hudson River is, at times, very good for striped bass.

When I was growing up, pollution wasn't an issue, and it was assumed that anything you caught was okay to eat. If I were to walk down Prospect Avenue without any clothes on, I'd probably light up because pollution was not something I worried about. We'd catch them and we'd eat them. We still catch them and eat them.

I do a lot of fishing now in the reservoirs around New York City. And as you launch your boat there's a big sign on the reservoirs: Do not eat one meal of fish from this pond in a week or a month or whatever. But at seventy-one I can't be worried about that. I don't care.

My Cub Scout and Boy Scout troop was in St. Augustine's Church. I started out as a Cub Scout when I was eight or nine, and although I never got to Eagle Scout, I must have stayed in the movement till I was fifteen or sixteen. We had some very big-time scoutmasters. Clarence Cave, who became a minister, was one of my scoutmasters. Walter

Bowen was another leader. Edler Hawkins, the civil rights activist, was the minister at the time. And we had a lot of youth activities at that church. We had a competitive basketball team called the Knights, and we'd play other teams. I'm not really sure how we did that because the ceiling of the gym was only about ten feet high.

Mostly I was a fisherman. I didn't get wrapped up in basketball or baseball or any other things. I just fished, because in fishing there's a variety of things you can do, and it's kind of contemplative. I don't mind sitting for an hour waiting for something to bite. I like being in places that are attractive botanically. I've got lots of patience, and I get a kick out of catching stuff.

I eventually became a nature counselor at Camp Minisink, so I taught other people about nature, the plants, the trees, the trails, the spotted turtles that are an endangered species there. I also taught them about the snapping turtles, the green snakes, the water snakes.

Crotona Park Lake has always been a mystery to me. There is no apparent inlet or outlet. I don't know where the water comes from. I don't know where it goes. All I know is that when I first started fishing there, we used to use a bent straight pin with a thread, and we used either worms or pieces of dough, and we'd catch sunnies—sunfish. That went on for years. After a while we discovered that there were catfish in there that were bigger than the sunnies, so they were better for the table. Then there were these crawfish, and the crawfish taste pretty good in the pot. We didn't talk pollution. We just said this is where you catch whatever.

At Minisink, I used rowboats to fish. Canoes are too unsteady for me. I think that if you want to be in a canoe you should just canoe, but you can't use a canoe to fish because sometimes you hook something that's really substantial, and if you're not paying attention you get dunked. I don't like being in the water.

Being a nature counselor encouraged me to be a science teacher. All my life I'd been interested in science. I went to Hunter College, where I studied science, and I ended up working at Sloan-Kettering Institute for Cancer Research as a lab technician. My sister Bessie was working as a gym teacher at Alexander Burger Junior High School, a school in the Bronx near St. Mary's Park. That was mostly Puerto Rican in those years.

At the time, I was making $2,800 a year. We had to work every day at Sloan-Kettering. We got time off, but we had to follow the experiments, and when the experiment was due, you had to be there. They'd give you the time in days, and so I worked at Burger as a substitute teacher. Then my sister lobbied for me to get to be a full-time teacher there.

My first full-time teaching position was as a science teacher. I came in January on a full-time contract and I had class 9–9. In those days they graded kids based on their academic achievement, for example on a scale from 9–1 to 9–16. I had class 9–9, and I learned more from those kids in 9–9 than I've learned before or since.

The first thing you have to learn as a teacher is how to manage the kids. I had a middle group in terms of achievement, and they were also middle in terms of behavior. We had to figure out how we were going to make this thing work. So we had a different kind of relationship. They were good to me, that class 9–9. I really appreciated that because they knew I was new and I knew that I didn't know how to manage them. So we helped each other.

Having been a camp counselor for a few years, I had a way of working with kids that seemed to work for me. I thought that I was fair, they thought I was fair, and we kind of collaborated on a lot of stuff. I worked with them to accomplish the task of learning and teaching as if they had something to contribute to that process. It wasn't that I'm the teacher sitting up here and there are the kids down there. I said, "Look, this is what we have to learn. Let's figure how we're going to go about doing it." It worked out well for me.

When I was teaching science, it was very hands-on, a gee-whiz kind of thing. I'd usually figure out some kind of a thing I would do, and the kids would say, "How did you do that?" One of the things we did was to take a ball and have it sit up on top of a water fountain. The kids liked to look at the ball and see that it wasn't falling off, that it was just sitting right at the top spinning around.

And we'd do things like putting hydrochloric acid in a bottle with metal filings, and it would create hydrogen gas and we'd light the gas coming out the tube, and they'd say, "That's interesting."

Fortunately, I have a little person who sits on my right shoulder and looks out for me. One time we were going to do that hydrogen experiment, and you know how the kids gather around the science table? I said, "Everybody move back." I lit whatever it was and everything exploded, but they were far enough back so they didn't get hurt, and this person on my shoulder looked out for me. We didn't do that experiment any more.

A couple of times we dissected things. I remember the last rabbit that I dissected for the class. That was an emotional experience for all of us because the rabbit was alive. We used ether to put the rabbit to sleep, and in the process the rabbit convulsed. It was the kind of thing you never forget, and so I haven't killed any more animals that way. I go to the place where they pickle them, and we get them dead.

I loved teaching. It was very tense and very trying and very hard, but I got along with the kids. After I made it through that first six months, I could do almost anything.

I still remember a kid named Thomas Manigault. We got along real well, and we managed the class together. It was wonderful. I don't re-member too many things from that long ago, but I remember him. One of those good kids who got what I was trying to do, and the other kids kind of went along with the program. So we had a good time.

Let me tell you another story. The second year I was there they made up a schedule where I had two classes at the same time. It was supposed to be a lecture period, and the classes were held in a small auditorium. My regular classroom was on the fourth floor, and the auditorium was on the first floor, so it was always a rush to get there on time. One day I was late. I think I was fifteen minutes late, and class was only forty minutes. I assumed that when I arrived, the class would be in disarray. But when I opened the door, the kids got to their feet and clapped. I'll never forget that. These sixty kids or whatever it was were so happy that I had showed up. I thought, "Goodness gracious, I can do anything."

I'd been at Sloan-Kettering for five years, taught in public school for seven years, and then I must have gone to Harlem Prep for a year. At Harlem Prep I'm minding my own business, when one day here comes a person who knows me from Camp Minisink. She said she was at Columbia, and they had a program that helps people get their doctor-ate. The department chairman was looking for somebody to work with him, and I should come over that afternoon and see him.

So she took me over to a man named Frizziani, who was chairman of a department in Columbia Teachers College. He said, "I've heard some things about you, and I'm prepared to offer you a job at Teachers College where you will take your Ed.D., and I'm prepared to offer you a two-year contract." He said the contract would take care of all my ex-penses in terms of the school, and he asked me what I'd need to provide for my family, because by this time I had a wife and a couple of kids. I said I needed $10,000 a year. He said I'd get $1,000 a month tax-free to work with him for two years. This was in 1970.

When the two years were up, and because of the way things go with doctoral degrees, I hadn't finished. But I'd finished the coursework, and I was working on the dissertation. So I went to Borough of Manhattan Community College, and I became chairman of the Department of Developmental Skills, which meant we managed English as a second language and the remedial reading department.

I didn't have any experience in those areas. But I had some experience as an administrator because when I was at Burger the principal had made me acting assistant principal for a year.

The beginning of my second year at Manhattan Community College, President Draper called me into his office and reminded me that I hadn't gotten my degree. I told him I didn't need a degree to work there because it was a community college. Then he said, "Here's the deal. It's eleven o'clock in the morning. At three o'clock this afternoon you will sign an agreement that you will finish your degree by June 30, or you'll be fired as of the end of the semester." This was like April.

At quarter to three, his secretary calls me up and says, "Hey, I got these two letters. One is a conditional reappointment based on whether or not you finish the degree, and the other one is a termination. You come down here and sign whichever one you like."

So I get on the phone with my advisor at Teachers College. I say, "Hey, I got a problem. They said if I don't finish I'm out of a job."

So a guy named Jim Kelly, who was a part-time professor at Teachers College, said to me, "Every Monday at four o'clock you come down here, and we're going to get you through this degree." And every Monday we sat down and we went through what we had to go through. By June, I had a final draft of my dissertation.

I was lucky that in growing up I had so many mentors, including male mentors, which is something many young people today don't have. My first mentor was Pop Nevilles. We didn't think of him as a mentor; we just thought of him as a fishing counselor. And as I grew older there was another guy, Dudley DeCosta Cobham. He went to Lincoln University and got my brother James into Lincoln. He was one of the directors of Camp Minisink.

Another guy was Frizziani, who really helped me in terms of him being the chairman of a department at Teachers College. But the one who saved me was Jim Kelly, who was the one who said, "okay, sit down and let's figure this thing out." And there are lots of people who helped along the way. One guy who had a big impact on me came along when I'd finished my masters' degree at NYU. That was my first master's, the master's in science education. My advisor looked me in the eye, and he said, "You have enough education now." I didn't like that particularly, so I just said okay. Then I went on to Teachers College and got a master's in education, a six-year certificate in education administration, and an Ed.D. I got five college degrees. So that person was a mentor, but he didn't know it.

And when I was growing up on Prospect Avenue, there were people who helped kids with things or told them when they were out of line. There was a group called the Six and Sevens, for the six- and seven-year-olds. I was five years old, but they let me be in that club. So even early on there was a neighborhood organization that looked after little kids.

My mother was a club person. She was the cooperative fund chairperson for Camp Minisink for twenty-five years. My father was a commissioner of the Boy Scouts of New York City for a long time. And both of them were involved with Grace Congregational Church. My mother also had a bridge club and a club called the EX9—the Exclusive 9—that was a neighborhood club. One of the members was a woman named Prescovia McConney. When the club met at our house, we had to go upstairs and go to bed, because they hung out all night. But Prescovia McConney had one of these rolling belly laughs. When she would laugh, oh, man, the room would light up, the house would light up, everything would light up. We always knew she was there because she could laugh like that.

My parents also started a Union and Prospect block association, and now I've been the chairman of the local historical association in my neighborhood, and I'm the chairman of the regional block association in Teaneck, New Jersey, where I live now. There are twelve block associations, and we have leadership meetings, and I'm the one who runs them.

That has a lot to do with what my parents thought was something you should do. You never give them credit for teaching you that sort of thing, but it kind of seeps in between the cracks.

Arthur Crier

Arthur Crier (1935–2004), a singer and songwriter, was one of the leading figures in doo-wop and rhythm and blues in Morrisania in the 1950s and 1960s and a major promoter of the musical heritage of the Bronx. He cofounded the *Morrisania Review*, a rhythm-and-blues revival group that brought together some of that neighborhood's premier singers.

I was born in Harlem, but I was raised in the Bronx. I grew up on Prospect Avenue near Jennings Street, where my family moved in the late 1930s.

My father was one of the first black postal workers to run a post office in New York City. He worked at the General Post Office, where he was a supervisor. Nearly all the black families who moved to Prospect Avenue during the thirties were headed by postal workers or Pullman porters.

For elementary school, I went to P.S. 23 on 165th Street on Tinton Avenue. There were a lot of other African American children at the school, but there were also Italians, Irish, a mixture of groups. But when I blinked, they were gone, because whites were leaving the neighborhood.

As kids we had a good time. We used to buy two-by-fours and skates and make our own little scooters. We had a lot of kite flying because the roof was where everybody hung out, flying the kites or having picnics. We played street games like ringolevio, box tag, cops and robbers, cowboys and Indians.

Stickball was the main game. The goal was hitting two sewers. We also played single-double-triple, which was where you threw a ball off the stoops or the steps. We called it single-double-triple because every bounce was a single, double, or triple. And slug, which is where the ball hits the ground before it hits the wall.

Being from a certain block was very important when I was growing up. Everybody knew each other and looked out for each other. You could leave your doors open. It was just a nice, nice situation.

Before we moved to Tinton Avenue, my family belonged to St. Augustine's Presbyterian Church. Our house eventually became the fellowship house of the church, and the Rev. Edler Hawkins lived next door to us. He was a kind of legendary figure in the community and a very good friend of my family.

When I was growing up, there was a lot of music in my family. My father sang in a quartet before he became a postal employee, and my parents both sang in a church choir.

I remember some of their favorite records—Ace Box, Count Basie, Duke Ellington, Sarah Vaughan, the Golden Gate Quartet, the Billy Williams Quartet, the Swanee Quintet, Wings Over Jordan. That type of stuff.

I was in love with radio station WJZ because they used to have barbershop quartets. My family also took me to the Apollo and the Paramount to see people like Count Basie and the Ink Spots.

My father was an air-raid warden. In the Second World War they'd have sirens, and when the sirens went off the air-raid wardens would have to come by because there'd be a blackout and they'd have to tell people to get in the house or turn off the lights. My father also did a lot of coaching and recreation work at St. Augustine's church.

I was a great athlete as a young man. My sport was baseball. But I didn't play on my high school team. I came up before they had Little League. We'd just throw a little twenty-five-cents party to get our base-ball caps and our uniforms. We did all that on our own.

I went to P.S. 51, which was a mostly black school. There were already gangs by the time I went there. There were the Slicksters on 166th Street between Prospect and Union, where St. Anthony of Padua is located. There was the Copiens, the Mutualistics from Jennings Street.

You knew you weren't going on their turf because you'd be in trouble. Unless you were a singer. If you were a singer, you could go wherever you wanted. But that's not what made me a singer. We hadn't even recorded yet; we were just doing talent shows. But if they knew you were singing, they kind of let you by.

I started singing around the age of fifteen when I was in junior high. I started with a group called the Heavenly Five. They sang gospel, and we used to go to church and pass the hat around. There were Franklin Douglass, Charles Richardson, Harold Richardson, and a guy named Charles Cobb, who was a great bass and who sang with the all-state, all-city choirs. The response when we sang was beautiful. We could tell by the money they put into the plate.

Before I graduated from high school, I decided to join the Navy. I went down to 346 Broadway, and they told me, "No, you've got to go up to Fordham Road." So I was walking there and saw this sign, "Join the Marines," and that's when I walked upstairs and joined the Marines.

I was seventeen when I went into the Marines and seventeen when I got out. I joined on October 28, and I got discharged November 21. What happened was that I was climbing over one of those barriers—we had to leap over them with our equipment—and I hurt my hip real bad so they discharged me. But my family was proud that I'd enlisted. This was 1952, during the Korean War, and that was an honorable thing to do.

The move from gospel into secular music happened a little later. I'd gone to elementary school with a boy named Garry Morrison. I hadn't seen him for years, but when I got out of the service, I ran into him, and it turned out he was involved in signing groups. He told me they were starting a group called the Gay Tones, and he'd like me to try out for the bass. So I went and tried out, and I got the job.

This was 1952. By this time rhythm-and-blues groups were starting to record. The Five Keys—we had idols then—they were out there. People were singing in the streets. The Ravens came out first, and then the Orioles, and they just took over. I think the Orioles were what made everybody want to sing.

All the black radio stations were playing these groups. Willie and Ray, Dr. Jive. When you came home from school or work, you turned on the radio right away to WWRL. I can't remember the names of all the programs, but there were four or five. They were hard to hear because they were all the way at the end of the dial.

When the Gay Tones started performing live, we'd perform at talent shows at P.S. 99. That was the Motown of the Bronx. We'd go there at night, listen to the music, or if you had a groove you could rehearse.

I played the mellophone in high school. I wanted a trumpet because that was the thing at the time. Nobody had mellophones. I took my instrument home on the school bus. But I never worried about anyone taking it. There were some bullies who, when my mother gave me a peanut butter sandwich to go to the movies, they'd come and take my sandwich. But I never felt like my life was in danger at any point.

At the P.S. 99 talent shows, they'd have maybe ten groups on an evening. But we never lost a talent show. Always came in first place. We got a great reputation in the neighborhood, and it spread beyond the neighborhood because P.S. 99 would take us on trips out to Jersey, where we'd meet other singing groups.

We were lucky. Gene Redd was our lead singer. He went on to manage Kool and the Gang, but his father was with Earl Bostic, and he was also with the Billie Williams Quartet at one time, so we didn't have any problem getting a recording deal. We didn't have to go around and audition.

Our first record came out in 1953. By then we'd changed our name to the Chimes because someone said our name made it sound like we were gay.

Our first record was "Dearest Darling." The first time we heard it played on the radio, oh, man, we jumped up and down in the room. We thought we were becoming stars, superstars. It was great.

Our first gig was with Charlie Parker, Lester Young, the Solitaires, and the Velvets at the Rockland Palace. Wherever there was a talent show, we were there. But our base was P.S. 99, and they had talent shows there every four or five months.

We couldn't support ourselves through the music, though. We were still seventeen, still living with our mommas.

Later on I got a job with Western Union, in the Empire State Building, which I loved. Even before that there was a guy, McEssen Roberts, who used to come around with a truck and go to different drugstores. This guy had me help him, so that was my first job, when I was fifteen. He'd pay me ten dollars to help him carry stuff to different drugstores.

We didn't compete on street corners with other singers in the doo-wop years. The talent shows were where we battled. When we sang on the corner, we'd sing with everybody. It wasn't necessarily my group against yours. It was just, if you saw three people, there was going to be some singing.

We never performed at any of the clubs in Morrisania, but I used to visit those places. Top jazz artists played at those clubs. I saw Gary Morrison, who was singing with my group, and later on he sang with Nancy Wilson. When she first came to New York she sang at the Blue Morocco. Nat King Cole's brothers played at Freddy's on 168th Street. I can't remember all the names, there were so many. Everybody came through, all really professional guys.

Morrisania was a tremendous place for music. We had Freddy's, the Blue Morocco, and the Apollo Bar about three blocks from each other on Boston Road. The Apollo Bar was between 168th Street and 169th Street. Right down the street on the corner was Freddy's, on 168th Street. Then across the street from them, close to 167th Street, was the Blue Morocco. People came to these places from all over. As a kid, I thought they would always last.

Tito Puente and Tito Rodriguez were on those shows. Tito Puente used to knock me out, and Tito Rodriguez too. They'd battle against each other in the dubs. And we danced to Latin music too, the mambo when the mambo came out and the Latin boogaloo. Five cents for the jukebox, and that was it.

In terms of audience enthusiasm, the period of doo-wop groups lasted all through the fifties and into the early sixties. When the Beatles and Motown came out, that kind of killed it. But we had about ten good years. I had a big hit in 1961, a song called "Nag" with a group called the Halos, and we got to travel all over the country.

I sang with a lot of different groups. But my main occupation was being a songwriter. The way it happened was, a boy named Robert Spencer, who sang with the Cadillacs, came up to me and said, "Man, if you go downtown, you can make some money writing songs." So that's how I became a songwriter.

We'd go down to 1619 Broadway, the Brill Building, and 1650 and 1697 Broadway. That's what you'd call Tin Pan Alley, those three buildings. We started from the top floor, and we knocked on doors. We'd knock on the door, go in, and sing our songs. And they'd say no, so we'd go to the next floor and they'd say no. And then the next floor, the guy said, "That's the greatest thing I've ever heard." So you've got to laugh because somebody will always like your stuff eventually.

From making the rounds like that I got to know everyone in the industry in New York, and I started doing background work. That's how I got to do "Pretty Little Angel Eyes" with Curtis Lee.

There was a group called the Cues, who were also black, but they didn't have the rawness we had. We had more of a raw thing that they wanted at the time, so everybody was hiring us. We did "Who Put the Bump in the Bump" and "Every Breath I Take" by Gene Pitney. We did the backups, but we also did the arrangements. When they hired us, they knew that we came in with ideas.

We didn't know anything about the publishing end of the business. We knew we got the advance from the songwriting, but we didn't know how to get our own publishing business going. We were in it for, well, the first thing was the girls. I discovered girls when I got in the Gay Tones, when I was seventeen. They changed my whole life.

By the time the sixties hit, we're doing arrangements, we're doing backup. I stayed in the music industry all through the late sixties. Then I went to Motown, and I worked for Motown as a songwriter and arranger. They set us up in an apartment in Detroit, and it was really nice.

The way that happened was through a guy named Al Cleveland. We needed a singer. We were in 1650 Broadway, and the singer we needed didn't show up, so we went to find people at the Brill Building because the Church Club was there, and a lot of musicians hung out at the Church Club. That's where you got your musicians from.

When you sold a song you had to make a demo, so if you sold a song to a publisher, he'd send you down [to] get some musicians to make a demo. So this day we needed a singer, and we saw this guy standing in front of 1619 Broadway with a suitcase and a marcel, so I figured he must be a singer. So I said, "Would you like to make some money? I mean, do you sing?" He said, "Yes, I sing." He'd been there about three months trying to make it as a singer. He came from Pittsburgh, and he was getting ready to go home, waiting for the Greyhound bus, and so he came up. He did the session and I told him, "You can live with me." I was living on 142nd Street at the time, so he moved in with me.

Anyway, he wound up writing "What's Going On" with Marvin Gaye and "I Second That Emotion" with Smokey. He sent for me, I had a group called the Gees, and he played one of our songs for Smokey. Smokey loved it and had me come to Detroit, and they signed me up. That was 1968.

My first steady work was with Shapiro and Bernstein. I'd been doing songwriting for some time, and Carlos Finch and I went to Shapiro and Bernstein. We had a song called "Turn the Page" that they loved, even though we had it with another publisher. And they signed us up. So we started making $150 a week, and we just had to bring in our music on Thursdays. So we had all the freedom in the world to do what we loved and get paid for it too. In those days, $150 a week was a lot of money.

I made the transition from performer to songwriter, arranger, performer, and manager. I managed many groups. I think I started managing between 1962 and 1968.

I learned how to do these things from experience, just from being around, seeing, observing. Then there was a fellow named Richie Barrett, who was a good friend of mine and who discovered Frankie Lyman and the Teenagers, Little Anthony and the Imperials, the Chantels, and the Three Degrees. He kind of hipped us about the business end of things. He's the one who really came out of the fifties with some money.

Before Motown, I was used to big studios in Manhattan. We had big, fabulous studios that we used. When I went to Motown and I saw the studio, it was in the basement of a private house. You go down to this little basement, and you say to yourself, "Wow, all these hits came from this little place." It blew my mind.

Berry Gordy, the one who started Motown, still had his hand in everything. It was like a music college, and Berry Gordy was the professor. When somebody brought in a song, they'd have a panel of songwriters, publishers, and salespeople, and they'd play the record, and they'd have a vote on it, up and down. Sometimes they'd say, "No, you need more bass," things like that. It was great. I mean, the man was fantastic. People talk about the Motown sound, but really, it was his business.

There's been a lot of publicity recently about Motown's studio musicians. In New York, everybody sang and played at once. The bands played and you sang, and it sounded good until you got home and listened to it, and you said, "Dag, it's not that good." And also, if somebody made a mistake, you had to start all over again.

But Gordy laid tracks. He had to lay tracks because the studio was so small that you couldn't fit everyone in there at once. He was the first one to do this. And when you lay tracks, it's much easier because all you have to do is concentrate on one thing at a time. You bring your rhythm in, and make sure that rhythm is straight, and then you take the singer and let the singer take it home, then you come back with the horns, and you put the horns on top of the rhythm.

Gordy lay tracks from the beginning because he figured he couldn't get the sound he wanted any other way. If he wanted to use horns, they would overload into other microphones. The studio was so small, the drummer had to go into another place and close the door. He was separated from the singers and musicians. That's why his sound was so good. He put the mics in there with him.

I stayed in Detroit until 1972. Then I went to a record company in Manhattan called Right On Records. That was a big mistake because they were really into cocaine, selling and dealing and all that. So I walked away from that after a while. One day I just left. I didn't even come to get my paycheck. But I never left the business.

In 1972, when I left Right On Records, I heard about a job in youth recreation in the Tremont neighborhood. They had all these gangs up there, and when I went for my interview, I saw this first hand. I went down into this basement on Bronx Park South, and they had this group called the Togetherness Block Association that was interviewing people for the job. The Black Assassins were down there, and they had their guns and everything, and they were just standing around while I was being interviewed. I think when they heard I was from Motown, that kind of influenced them, and I got the job.

It was supposed to be a sports and recreation program. But I decided to bring music into the program, and I gave a talent show. That night it was standing room only. After that, they elevated me to full time. I had a football team. I had a baseball team. And of course I kept doing the talent shows.

By then the Bronx was completely different from the way it was when I was growing up. It was just messed up; there were drugs and everything. But I figured I could change things. And I did. I had all those guys help me. I made the gang members ushers at the talent shows.

My first office was on Tremont, and later it was on 180th Street. We didn't have a big recreational facility, so we had them fix up the corner of 180th Street and Vyse Avenue for our basketball tournament. We had a basketball tournament that ran seven days a week. We had two Little League teams, the Demons and the Tigers. We had a Pony League team. We had a football team. And then we had the family day picnic. We went to Van Cortland Park, and I got money from different stores.

When I was running the talent shows, rap music was performed on stage. I promoted all those young groups because I knew a guy named Sal Abbatiello who owned Disco Fever, the bar on Jerome Avenue where all the hip-hop groups used to go. He asked me to manage the bar for him. All the early rappers performed there, the Funky Four, the Cold Crush Brothers, Afrika Bambaataa and his crew.

I knew the Cold Crush Brothers really well. When I lived in the Lambert Houses on 180th Street, they lived on my floor. They performed in my talent shows, and I have a picture of DJ Charlie Chase and Grandmaster Caz going with me to entertain the inmates at Rikers Island.

I took the winners of those talent shows to Rikers Island, and we went to hospitals to sing for senior citizens. I was still doing my youth programs and talent shows in the eighties when crack hit. At the time I was a youth coordinator for Mayor Koch. They had fifty-two youth coordinators in the city, and I was assigned to the Tremont area.

I started the Morrisania Review in 1994. It came out of a reunion of all the Bronx singing groups. We all came out of the Morrisania area, and everybody had a hit, so I reached out to all the guys who had had a hit and said, "Here's a way you can still have your own hit and work together to create a new audience."

In 1999, I organized a reunion of all the doo-wop groups. It was called Great Day in Harlem, it was on June 6, and it took place in Harlem. We took the picture on Strivers Row. We got the Chantels, the Cadillacs, and many more groups. It was a historic event.

I also had a show for Bronxnet public access TV called *Doo-Wop Is Alive* that started about thirteen years ago. I don't know when it's on because I live down South now, but I know I saw it this week on Monday and Tuesday. They show the reruns, and I get a lot of letters because people love it.

There's a huge following for this music. I did a New Year's Eve show on PBS with the Chords last year. They had a million-selling record, "Sh-Boom," in 1954. I think the Billie Williams Quartet had a hit with it, Stan Freberg had a comedy hit with it, there was a Latin record, naturally the Crew Cuts had a big hit, and Floyd had a hit. So you had five big records that year.

The only thing that's bad is that no one told the Chords to join BMI. If they'd joined BMI that year, they'd have been fat. So what happened is that their money started dwindling down, and then the TV show *Happy Days* came out, and now there's a five-way split, and they get at least eighty to ninety thousand apiece off of "Sh-Boom." That thing was crazy. That's what started bringing back that music.

Plus this lady Joan Jett, she covered my song "Nag," and it sold ten million copies. Ten million. I get royalties for that. In terms of my musical career, the song that brings me the most royalties is "Nag," because I wrote it and have the songwriter's credit.

The Chords opened the door to all this. They were the first crossover group, and "Sh-Boom" opened the doors for everybody. They were my buddies; we all hung out together. They wanted me to sing with them, but I was with my group, and I wouldn't go. I'm sorry now. There's only one member living now, but their families get all the royalties. And "Sh-Boom" makes a lot of money. It's been in all kinds of movies, cartoons, everything. *The Texas Chainsaw Massacre*, it opens up with playing "Sh-Boom." So it's a big song.

Even though I moved down South, I'm still involved in a million projects. I did a big show down in Warsaw, North Carolina, where I live. I called it "the biggest talent show ever given in Warsaw." The local newspaper devoted two full weeks of articles to the show. I've got a band down there now, a rhythm band, and I'm getting ready to do some recording. I'm also going to be recording some singers from my talent show, and singing some doo-wop down in South Carolina.

In the little town of Warsaw, there was no place for kids to go. There's no stage for them. If I want to go to Wal-Mart, I have to go fifteen miles. There's nothing in my town, really. Piggly Wiggly, that's our neighborhood supermarket.

Gene Norman

Gene Norman (1935–), an architect, designer, and urban planner, is a former chairman of the New York City Landmarks Preservation Commission.

When my family first moved to the Bronx, to an apartment on Claremont Parkway and Third Avenue, my parents had broken up, and my father didn't live with us. We lived with my grandparents, and my grandfather was a superintendent of the building we lived in.

It wasn't a predominantly Jewish neighborhood, although a lot of Jewish people lived there. But there were also Italians. I remember going to the food market on Bathgate Avenue and seeing all types of goodies and people.

This was the first time my grandfather worked as a super. Before then we lived on the Lower East Side. I think what happened is that he was the one who got the job, and my family moved with him.

I went to P.S. 2, which is a little north of Morris High School and next to a brewery which I think was called the Rheingold Brewery in those days. You could see the plumbing and the huge copper vats from the Third Avenue El. This was right before World War II, and the neighborhood was becoming more black than white.

This area, around the intersection of Boston Road and Third Avenue, was pretty heavily an African American neighborhood. And when we moved to Home Street and Union Avenue, that area was also predominantly black at that time.

I made my first communion at Our Lady of Victory on Webster Avenue. I must have been five or six. When we moved further east, I began going to St. Anthony of Padua on 166th Street and Prospect Avenue, a parish that was about fifty-fifty black and white in those days.

I think my family moved around a great deal when I was a child. That's just speculation on my part. But in talking to older members of the family, it seems that when the war started there was a lot of competition among property owners to get tenants and so they'd offer certain inducements like cheaper rent or a fresh painting to get people to rent houses.

On Home Street we lived in a private house, and when we moved to Prospect Avenue, which was perhaps a year later, we moved into another private house. It was a back house, if you know what that means. There was a house on Prospect Avenue, and there was an alley between that house and its next-door neighbor. You walked down the alley, and once you got past the first house there was an open area with grass and trees and two more houses. We lived in one of those.

My mother and grandparents stressed education. You had to do well at school. Plus I was an only child, so all the attention was focused on me. I can't honestly say that I showed artistic talent at an early age. That doesn't mean I wouldn't try to do things like draw, but I didn't think I was very good. I was good with my hands, though. I used to make things. In those days model making was an activity you spent time on.

Coming from a West Indian background, as I did, children are to be seen and not heard and spoken with. You didn't inject yourself into conversation. But there had been a lot of talk about the Marcus Garvey movement during the late twenties and early thirties when my grandparents first came to New York. There was also a lot of talk about the racial situation in the United States. If a black man got lynched down South, the adults would talk about that as a terrible event, and I as a child would have some understanding of what had happened.

Most of the people who visited us were West Indian, but the food served was more eclectic. My grandmother used to take cooking jobs for non–West Indians, and through that she learned other dishes. For example, she made a great corned beef and cabbage.

My mother worked for a while as a maid, and later she became a practical nurse. And I knew about the Bronx slave market, the corner of Westchester Avenue and Southern Boulevard where African American women would be picked up by employers. I never heard it called the slave market, but there were people—mostly women, but men used to be there as well—looking for what they called day work.

I attended P.S. 23, but I don't have much memory of that school. I don't think I was there more than one or two grades. Because of where it was located on Tinton Avenue near 168th Street, most of the kids who went there were black. When I moved from that neighborhood to Kelly Street, most of the kids in my classes were not black.

These schools were tracked by ability level. As far as I remember, they determined who was in each track through standardized testing. I remember taking all sorts of tests through the years. I was always in the so-called 1 class. The racial composition of the 1 classes was different from the racial composition of the 6 classes. In the 1 class there were very few minorities. The higher the number, the more blacks and Hispanics.

When we moved to Kelly Street, and I started P.S. 39 in the third grade, there must have been perhaps thirty kids in the class. Of those thirty children there were probably four or five black and Hispanic boys and a like number of girls. The rest were primarily Jewish, and there were some Italians. Colin Powell lived across the street from me, and we were very close. He was my best friend.

We lived for a short time on Kelly Street between 163rd and Intervale. But the block we lived on the longest was between 163rd and Westchester Avenue. On one side of the block there were four-story tenement walkups. On the other side, the side I lived on, there were large apartment houses with at least twenty apartments per building.

When I lived on that block, it was multiethnic, but there weren't many blacks. I'm talking about the years from 1944 through 1953, when I went into the military. In the beginning there were a lot of Jewish families, but after the war they moved away, and a lot of Hispanic families moved in.

We played games on a seasonal basis. Say it was spring, we'd play marbles. We'd play ball games—box ball, curb ball, off-the-wall ball, stickball. In the summer when we weren't in school we'd play baseball, but that was at a place quite a ways away. In the fall we'd play touch football in the street, or we'd go to a park or a vacant lot and play tackle football.

There were a couple of vacant lots in the neighborhood, perhaps where buildings had burned down, and we used to roast marshmallows and sweet potatoes there. There was a market block on 168th Street with a string of food stores, and we'd go there to beg, borrow, or steal sweet potatoes, things of that nature. In the fall we'd make little bonfires on those lots or in the street. In those days there weren't as many cars in the streets, so the streets doubled as a playground—a fairly safe playground, I should add. And we'd build these little fires and roast our potatoes.

I also went to movies at the drop of a hat. To get money, we'd collect bottles and turn them in. You could get five cents for a cork bottle and three cents for a twelve-ounce bottle. We'd go around to our neighbors, collect the bottles, and then go off to the movies on a Saturday.

The closest movie theater was the Tiffany. It wasn't a first-run movie house. You had to wait maybe two or three weeks after a picture had played in the other local houses to see it, but you got three movies, cartoons, coming attractions, and a newsreel for twenty-five cents. We also used to go a few blocks further to the so-called first-run movies—first run meaning in the neighborhoods, not downtown in the Times Square area—to Loew's Boulevard and the Loew's Spooner.

These were on Southern Boulevard, on two blocks between Westchester and 163rd Street. It was our mall, I suppose, by today's standards. There were actually three movie theaters—the third one was called the Star—and occasionally we'd go there. We didn't like the Star, though, because it had mean matrons, those women in their forties or older who wore white nurses' uniforms, carried flashlights, and told us rowdy kids to keep quiet.

In addition to food stores, that block had all the retail outlets—clothing, shoes, jewelry, gifts. You name it, it was on that block. There were three five-and-dime stores there—Woolworth's, Kress, and Grant's. So when we had nothing to do, we'd walk up to the Boulevard, as we used to call it, and do window shopping and just see what was out there.

As we grew older, we also went to Manhattan. We'd go to museums; we'd go to events in Central Park. Right after the war I remember going to a big exhibition of military things in the park, and we went down to see the trucks and the tanks. We'd occasionally go with our families to a movie downtown. That was a big deal because you had to get dressed up.

I don't remember what I'd call racial tension in the neighborhood when I was a child, but there were incidents that were initiated by some sort of racial comment.

My block was a mixed block, but others were not. The block between Intervale and Longwood Avenues, where P.S. 39 is, was totally black. Dawson Street, which was nearby, was also totally black. And from time to time there would be arguments. They didn't start racially, but race surely got into it. In those days, as kids became teenagers they formed stickball teams. The different stickball teams would play each other, block against block, and they'd usually play what was called a money game. The players and their supporters would put up money to bet on the game, and there would be some dispute about where a ball was hit, or who dropped it, or who caught it. And because you might be on someone else's block, you sometimes thought, "What do you think, that we're going to take this from you?"

There would be some sort of scuffle, and invariably words would be exchanged in a heated situation, and sometimes people would say things to each other about race. But they were passing incidents. There wasn't an atmosphere of racial problems.

My mother and grandmother talked openly about what to do when encountering racially charged situations. At an early age, you understood that there was a difference between blacks and whites, a double standard, and that you didn't do certain things without a consequence or a problem resulting from it. They'd tell me, don't let anyone push you around no matter who they are. Don't get involved with white policemen because they won't give you a fair shake. I don't remember being told not to go to certain areas, but I was told that you had to be aware and alert no matter where you went, so just watch it.

For the most part, the teachers were fair to everyone. At P.S. 39, I thought they were pretty fair, but at J.H.S. 52, which was a much larger grouping of kids, with kids from further away from our neighborhood, the situation was a little different. The school was on Kelly Street between Avenue Saint John and Leggett Avenue. When it got time to be thinking about high school, they let only three people take the test for the Bronx High School of Science. I was one of the three. The other minority kids weren't allowed to take the exam for Stuyvesant High School, and I thought there was some racial prejudice going on there.

I also remember gangs in the South Bronx in the forties. They started out as athletic teams, but after World War II the whole neighborhood changed. Returning soldiers started coming home. Some of them were young people who had been in combat situations, and they tended to group together.

So there was this older group of guys. The next step down on the hierarchy would be the teenage kids in high school, and below that would be kids like me who just were starting junior high. So there were these three groupings, and each group had some sports affiliation, like a team. As time went on there were rivalries among these groups, and I think that was the root of the so-called gang activity.

Around junior high school there would be problems, where for whatever reason people in the school got into a fight. The news got around very quickly. And the next day, if the guys came from different neighborhoods or blocks, they'd bring their friends to either witness or participate in a new fight.

I don't remember being fearful. But I remember an incident on my block in the early fifties where somebody's sister had been insulted by somebody, and she went home and told her brother, who got in touch with some group from around St. Ann's Avenue. Next thing you know, that night a moving truck pulls into the block. Forty or fifty guys came out of the truck with pipes and clubs and who knows what, maybe knives and guns, and they were going to find this person and if he had any friends, they'd find them too. I don't remember how it ended up.

Morris High School, when I was there, was mixed racially. The school was in a neighborhood that was almost 100 percent black, but it was zoned so that kids from the Hunts Point area and places toward the east had to go to Morris. They'd come by public bus because there were no school buses in those days unless you were handicapped or something. So here was an example of where white kids were bused into a black school, which is the reverse of what went on later on in this country. But we got along; I don't remember there being any racial animosity.

When I entered Morris, I was aware that my goal was to go to college. I was in the so-called academic group. No one said it, but it was expected that anyone in the academic program would go to college. And the classes we were given and the makeup of the students in the class all pointed in that direction.

When it comes to the music I listened to when I was young, there's a special issue for black Americans in this country in the sense that we have to know two cultures at the same time and weave them together. Sometimes three cultures. I like to think I was exposed to three cultures and was able to keep them all in the air and cross over whenever needed.

One was the West Indian–based culture with calypso music. Then there was the black American or Negro culture, as it was called in those days, and that was primarily based on Southern traditions and music—the blues and a little bit of jazz. My mother remarried in 1946, and my stepfather had come from Virginia, so I was exposed to gospel music when a lot of other West Indians didn't know anything about gospel music. At the same time I was exposed to the top twenty or top forty, whatever it was called in those days, so you'd hear the commercial music. I was also exposed to classical music, and I listened to live music because my family used to go to these fraternal organizations for parties and dances. I don't remember the names of the organizations, but it was always the benevolent society of you name it, the sons and daughters of wherever.

I have the best recollection of the Hunts Point Palace because in the fifties, when I was in high school, the Hunts Point Palace was the mecca for Latin and mambo music, as it was called, not just in the Bronx but in the city. All the big bands would play there for fairly cheap admission—Tito Puente, Tito Rodriguez, Noro Morales, Pacheco.

I also remember the Hunts Point Ballroom. That was over near Morris High School, and from time to time some group would be giving a dance or something, and we'd go there. But the dances I was talking about, the West Indian dances, were not in the Bronx. They were in Harlem. For blacks Harlem still functioned as a major reference point, where you went for cultural reasons, fraternal reasons, visits. It was where most people came from, so going there was like going back home.

We had friends who lived in Harlem still, and we would go to visit them. And we'd go to dances at the Rockland Palace, the Renaissance Ballroom, Park Palace, any number of different venues.

I started getting interested in Latin music when I was ten or twelve. Kelly Street, where I lived then, became a magnet for Latin musicians. There was a band headed by a guy named Noro Morales, whose mother lived on our block. He'd come visit his mother and bring his friends, and Tito Puente and Tito Rodriguez and these guys would hang out on the roof of the buildings and play music on a Sunday afternoon with their bongos and drums.

So I grew up with the bongos, but they didn't have the negative connotation that the bongo noises have now. I mean, these guys were good.

Then there was this nightclub on Westchester Avenue not far from us called the Tropicana Club, named after the Tropicana Club in Havana, Cuba. I remember as a kid on a summer night hearing the trumpet riffs of the mambo band floating through the air like a pied piper's tale.

This was part of the soundtrack of my life. In those days, as the neighborhood became more and more Hispanic, music took on a greater and a more engulfing place in your life. Music seemed to be everywhere.

In the late forties drugs started coming into the community. There was a place down in Lexington, Kentucky, where you were sent for what you'd call drug treatment today, to rehabilitate yourself and somehow decriminalize yourself. We had a couple of people a year or so, people older than me, who had been there and came back. They'd been sent there because they'd been arrested for smoking marijuana.

As in most criminal situations, you start out with something small like smoking marijuana, and you get thrown in with people who are bigger offenders. It's like the purse snatcher getting thrown in jail with the bank robber, and before you know it he knows how to rob banks. These couple of people from our block came back, and there is such a subculture and language about using drugs, and some people want to be part of an organization or a lifestyle or whatever and were drawn to this. And little by little the marijuana graduated up to heroin, which became the major drug.

In the fifties when I was in high school, we must have lost a good dozen people that we knew of to overdoses of heroin. These were kids who six months before you were playing stickball with or going to the movies with. And six months later they are so involved with drugs that they overdose.

After the war, people started moving away from the Bronx. The suburbs started getting developed, and Charlie Wilson—he's one of the villains I like to point to, he heads up General Motors, but gets appointed as secretary of defense—promotes the idea of a national defense highway system. So now highways are being built to move people away from the cities into places that were impossible in terms of commuting to work. Long Island, for example, becomes developed, developers build tract housing, and people begin to move out of the city into these areas, leaving behind a kind of vacuum.

When I graduated high school, I was barely seventeen. When I started that fall at Hunter College, I was seventeen and six months or so. I wasn't emotionally prepared for college. Hunter, which is now Lehman College, was an idyllic, tree-lined, ivy-covered place where there were maybe four female students to every male student. It had just begun accepting males. And it was like being a rooster in a henhouse. I just felt that I needed to grow up some more. So in 1953 I went into the Marines. It was a big decision, and I am glad I made it. Plus, to be totally honest, my grades weren't that good.

People played numbers all the time. And not just on Kelly Street. Every neighborhood I lived in, there was a numbers runner. I always marveled at how they could keep all that numerical information and names of people straight without writing anything down. But they had to do it that way because if the police ever caught them, they didn't want to have slips on them.

This was mostly nonviolent. Occasionally a numbers runner might get stuck up. But it was so local and so quick that whoever did it would be known in a minute and be severely dealt with.

On Kelly Street, a great many of the women in the families did not work and stayed at home. So there were a lot of adults monitoring the behavior of young people. As time went on it diminished because more and more new people moved into the block as the middle-class people [were] moving out. But in the beginning you were subject to [be] reprimanded by any adult on the block if you stepped out of line. Which meant that you would probably get two good smacks: one from the adult who stopped you, and that adult would tell your parents, and you'd get another one.

When I got back to Kelly Street in 1956, it was very different than it had been in 1953. There had been a lot of turnover, and there were so many new faces around that I felt like a stranger. Colin Powell's family moved to Queens in 1956, and his family wasn't the only one that chose to move. The neighborhood had become an area that looked unsafe and felt unsafe. You could see and feel the difference because what you'd been used to did not exist. And there were a great many newcomers who were Hispanic and spoke little English. They were called hillbillies or "jibaro" by Hispanics who had been there before and spoke English. These people just seemed alien.

Plus there was all this drug traffic. It wasn't like 24/7, mind you, but

if you knew where to look for it, you could see it. You could see someone nodding off, and you'd just know.

When I was in high school I had three ambitions: I thought about
being a pharmacist because I'd gotten to know the pharmacist in the
drugstore on the corner, and I thought that was kind of interesting. I
thought about being a science person—exactly what was unclear—and
I thought about being a history teacher. I was very interested in history,
and I still am.

When I started Hunter College I was a science major and I had
thoughts of possibly teaching. It wasn't until I was in the Marine Corps
that I got to see the greater world thanks to different training assignments. We were sent to Puerto Rico—to Vieques, of all places—and
we got to see a whole different type of building than I'd been used to.
When I got out, I thought that being an architect sounded like a good
thing to be. When I was in high school I didn't even know the word
"architect." I knew that engineers designed and built things, but never
architects.

When I started on this career path after coming back from the Marines, it was trial and error, at least in the beginning. My first job was
working as a messenger at a large architectural firm. In those days, that
was one of the routes you could follow if you hadn't finished school.
It was normal that in a year or so you'd be promoted to be a junior
draftsman, which is what happened in my case. My first boss took a
liking to me and allowed me to gain experience and come along. It was
a large firm with over five hundred employees, but I was responsible for
projects after about two and a half years.

It wasn't a typical architectural firm because it also had engineers.
Most firms hire consulting engineers, someone to do the electrical and
someone to do the plumbing and so on. In this firm everything was
all under one roof. There must have been ten or fifteen black people
working there, and I was one of the few who was given that sort of
responsibility.

I remember my boss taking me to see the head draftsman when I
was assigned to do a project for the first time. The head draftsman said
to me, "Do you think you can tell these old white guys what to do on
a project and have them do it? Because Eddie is recommending to me
that is what you are to do." And I said, "Sure. I used to be a sergeant
in the Marine Corps, and that's about how you deal with people." He

thought that was a pretty good answer, and that was the time I got to get a lead on a project.

I remember one time during the sixties, when I'd been there five years or so, and they started doing so much government work that they had to adhere to the government guidelines about nondiscrimination. There had been complaints that the firm had never promoted anyone to the title of project architect. There were people like me and one other person who were doing that job, but because we were black we didn't get that title.

I met my wife before I joined the Marine Corps. She lived across the street from me on Kelly Street, and she was of Puerto Rican ancestry. Matches like that weren't uncommon. Being West Indian, Caribbean, there's a lot of mixing of peoples. That's one of the traits of the rainbowing of being Caribbean.

When we got married, we moved to Simpson Street, which was three blocks from Kelly Street. This particular block was longer than our other block, and it had five six-story tenements on it. It seemed darker because you couldn't see the sky as easily as you could on our old block.

Our next stop was the Monroe Houses, where we moved in 1961, the year it opened and the year after my son was born. I'd put in for a public housing slot, and they had just finished the Monroe Houses in Soundview, which was south of Bruckner. It was a combination of building heights. Maybe half the buildings were eight stories, and the others were high-rises. It was a brand-new community, and we were the first tenants. The streets around us weren't even paved yet.

I thought of public housing as a step up because there were new appliances, and all the apartments were laid out so that there was light and air. There was also a screening process. They tried to integrate the project by placing a black family on each floor so there wasn't a whole floor of all blacks or all whites. It was multiethnic by design, by calculation and manipulation.

But this system started to break down the day after it opened. Something happened at the Housing Authority. They didn't keep being as careful about the selection process, or maybe they didn't have enough applicants or staff. But as people moved out—and people did move out—their replacements weren't handled as carefully as the original group. So little by little you'd find that there would be a whole floor or a whole building of one type of person, usually minority. It also seemed that the people coming in were less scrupulous about caring for the grounds.

My two younger children were born when we lived in the Monroe Houses. But eventually we left and moved to the Fordham Hill co-ops, a Mitchell Lama development. I felt that there was a distinct difference in the atmosphere there because in a co-op people had more of a vested interest in what was going on. You took more interest in knowing your neighbors, there was a socialization going on, kids got to know each other. It was more like a big extended family.

And by the time we left the Monroe Houses, it was becoming dangerous. The maintenance had fallen off dramatically. The number of kids and the noise they would generate increased considerably. My neighbors were people I didn't want to associate with.

After I came back from the Marines, I began to notice very dramatic physical deterioration in the neighborhood where I'd grown up. In any property-owning situation, there needs to be maintenance. Broken windows need to be fixed. Things need to be painted. The owners of those properties were either getting older or sold them off to others who didn't care. For a while, the fellow who owned our building lived in the building. So he always took care and was concerned about what was going on in the building. And that was a twenty-family building.

His name was actually Kelly. Old Man Kelly. When we first moved to Kelly Street and up to when I went into the Marines there were curtains on the vestibule doors. There were awnings on the building across the street. People shined the brass: that was the superintendent's job. Garbage was collected, sidewalks were swept and repaired. Then none of that was happening. You could see where the upkeep had slacked off.

By this time I was an adult. I'd seen a little of the world in the military. I'd gone to college and been stimulated by new ideas. I had a better sense of what America should be doing for people. I'd voted a couple of times. And what I wanted to see happen in this country wasn't happening on Kelly Street.

Instead, it became a dumping ground for people who were encouraged to come to this country to do menial work and often not finding this work, putting up with harsh cold winters, getting on relief, having more children than they needed to have, if I can be blunt, and just being a drain. Plus the owners of the buildings cared mostly about whether you paid rent. They didn't care about the buildings; they took no pride in the neighborhood.

By 1972, the Kelly Street I knew was a wasteland. People started moving out. Then in order to buy drugs, characters would come in and rip out plumbing lines. And more people moved out because when you see that around you, you want to leave. Somewhere in the late sixties, and certainly by the seventies, I used to take my kids by there to see it. The block was still standing, but it was vacant, like so many other neighborhoods in the Bronx.

This was something that was clearly happening in other blocks in that community. These nice buildings were all gone by the mid-seventies, replaced by some sort of public housing thing that has a street wall with no entrances on it.

Of all the buildings I grew up with, just two are still left on that block. When Colin Powell became famous, he told people that they should talk to me about his childhood. They did, and all the television interviewers said they wanted to see Kelly Street. "Where's the place that Colin Powell grew up?" they'd ask. And when I took them there, I took them to a parking lot because the parking lot is part of the housing development they had put up there.

When I saw all this, my first reaction was, I'm glad I moved out of there. My second reaction was, it's not just this block; it's the whole Bronx south of the Cross Bronx Expressway, which was being built when I was in the Marine Corps. So in that ten-year period between 1955 and 1965 the Bronx was devastated, and no one seemed to care. Could people have fixed it? I don't know. These are the same years the Vietnam War was building up, so it's all intertwined.

My understanding of how things work tells me it's not an isolated problem. It's not limited to just the Bronx; it is affected by the economy and world events and so on. But if you want to look at it from the Bronx point of view, at the same time this is happening they're building Co-op City. I remember taking my oldest son to Freedomland, which was on the site where Co-op City was built. Freedomland, which opened in 1960, was going to be modeled after Disneyland.

So Co-op City started in the late sixties, and people were encouraged to move there. The West Bronx didn't have too many young people, but the parents of the younger generation were occupying large apartments on the Grand Concourse. They were encouraged to move to Co-op City, and they did. So there were more and more vacancies, more and more vandalism, and more and more fires, so much so that they showed them on national television during the World Series. All we were left with was total devastation.

A lot of people started to do things about it by the time the seventies arrived. You remember President Jimmy Carter's famous visit to Charlotte Street. My grandmother owned a building around there, and my wedding reception, in 1959, was held in a catering hall on Boston Road and Bristol Street, right near my grandmother's building. I remember who ran it, a little West Indian group from the Virgin Islands called the Three Brothers of St. John. They rented it out for parties.

But what happened in that fifteen-year period was that everything slipped downhill, and only a couple of groups tried to do something about it. Father Louis Gigante over at St. Athanasius Church did some reclamation of older buildings near the church because if a church doesn't have people around it, there's no need for the church.

I lived in the Bronx, but I worked upstate and in Harlem. When I first started with the New York State Urban Development Corporation, I was in charge of the group that was handling housing and community development outside of New York City and in Rochester and Buffalo. And we built thousands of units of housing.

The place where we lived at the time, the Fordham Hill co-ops, was different from the area we came from. There were certainly problems. I had kids in school, and I knew there was starting to be drug trafficking in schools. I lived across the street from a junior high, and I heard that they had to have a policeman out there.

But I was able to protect my children in terms of the schools they went to. I was fortunate and lucky. Fortunate that I had a job that let me do some things. Lucky in that my oldest son went to Horace Mann High School. It's a funny story. Irv Gikofsky, the weatherman they called Mr. G, was a teacher at P.S. 131 in the Bronx, and my son was in his class. That's how my son got interested in meteorology, and that's what he does today.

At the same time, Irv was always looking out for ways to help these kids. My son was in the fourth or fifth grade, and he said there was this thing called Hilltop Schools Initiative, organized by the private schools in Riverdale to attract high-performing minority students, and I should fill out the papers and get him to take the test. My son passed the test, but then we had to figure out how to pay for it. We paid some and got a scholarship to Horace Mann School. From there he went to to MIT, and then to the graduate school at the University of Maryland. If you're lucky, good things can happen.

If you look at Kelly Street today, there's not a block left. It's just fragments of a block. On one side of the street you have a housing project that doesn't even have an opening to the street. So if you walk down the street, you're looking at a wall. They don't have a vibrant neighborhood of shops and activities. They don't have a mixture of people from different backgrounds to stimulate them, and they clearly don't have the kind of schooling I had.

I had good teachers who cared and pushed me. Now did they push everybody? I don't know. I don't think so. They probably pushed the kids who, based on test results, they thought would be the most successful, and if you weren't a good test taker you ended up in class 7–12, where they were just happy if you didn't stab them or bring a knife to school or your zip gun.

I see some progress, and that's good, but not enough progress. Still, I was exposed to the beginnings of that. It was like looking at something through a fog and the wind would blow and it would be like, "I see something moving out there." But we're talking about 1950, 1951, and not much was going on in those days.

James Pruitt, his brother Henry, and their father, Henry Pruitt Sr., on the stoop next to their family brownstone on East 168th Street in Morrisania. Their father, a postal worker, purchased the brownstone in 1940. The photo was taken in the mid–1940s.

St. Augustine's Presbyterian Church was an important center of spiritual, cultural, and intellectual life for the black Morrisania community. Its pastor, Reverend Edlar Hawkins, mentored several generations of Morrisania youth and brought figures like Duke Ellington and the Reverend Martin Luther King Jr. to the church.

Thessalonia Baptist Church's was the largest black congregation in the Bronx. Its charismatic leader, Reverend James Polite, moved the church into this beautiful synagogue building in 1943, marking Morrisania's transition from a largely Jewish to a predominantly black neighborhood.

Daphne Moss (Johnson) upon her graduation from Bellveue School of Nursing in 1969. She had a long and distinguished career both as a nurse and a health educator and as an administrator in the New York City Public Schools system.

Basketball great Nate "Tiny" Archibald, Victoria Archibald-Good, James Blakeney, and Dr. Harry Good at a Patterson Houses reunion. Nate, Victoria, and James all grew up in the Patterson Houses and have great memories of their childhood years there.

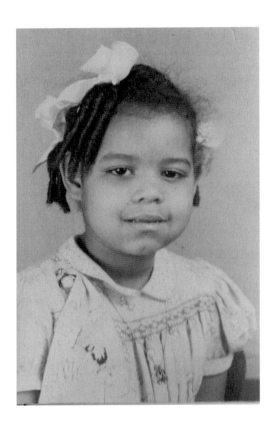

Andrea Ramsey in 1947 when she was living on Union Avenue in Morrisania. Her family was part of a large group of people of West Indian ancestry to move to Morrisania, along with African Americans, in the 1930s and '40s.

Joe Orange and his wife, Donna Orange, at their home in Maryland. Joe, who grew up on East 168th Street in Morrisania, was a highly successful jazz trombonist before he pursued a career in health care management.

Daphne Moss Johnson grew up on a mostly Latino block, Simpson Street, on the border of Hunts Point and Morrisania. This photo, taken in the schoolyard of P.S. 20 in 1962, shows four of her friends: John Bermudez, Chicky Escobar, Manny Vargas, and Augustine ("Gus") Torres.

Publicity photo of the jazz trumpeter, composer, and educator Jimmy Owens with his favorite instrument. Jimmy, who grew up near Joe Orange and the Pruitt family on East 168th Street, has traveled the world as a musician and performed with some of the great jazz artists of our time.

Club 845, which opened in 1945 on Prospect Avenue just off 161st Street, was one of New York's great neighborhood jazz clubs. Many of the greats of the Bebop generation performed here, among them Miles Davis, Dizzy Gillespie, Charlie Parker, Dexter Gordon, and Thelonious Monk.

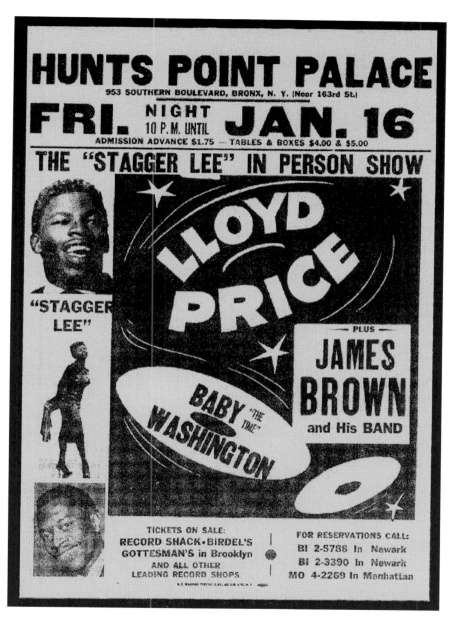

The Hunts Point Palace, located on Southern Boulevard south of Westchester Avenue, was the "Apollo of the Bronx." Not only did great black rhythm-and-blues stars such as James Brown perform here, it also featured the greats of Latin music, including many homegrown Bronx artists.

Boston Road between 166th Street and Prospect Avenue was the center of cultural and musical life in Morrisania from the early 1950s to the late '60s. The Blue Morocco and Freddie's were two of six clubs and theaters located on that strip, the Blue Morocco featuring Latin music and rhythm and blues, while Freddie's featured jazz.

Beatrice Bergland

Beatrice Bergland (1936–) is a retired corrections officer and a leader of the Community Church of Morrisania.

My family came to the Bronx in 1940, when I was about four. We moved from Bradhurst Avenue in Harlem to 1324 Grant Avenue, a few blocks from the Grand Concourse, and I went to P.S. 88, which was just around the corner.

P.S. 88 had its positive attributes. It was the only school I knew of that sent home the lunch menu so your parents could say what they wanted you to eat.

Back then the neighborhood was entirely Jewish, and as far as I knew, my brother and I were the only black children in the school. The Jewish kids used to chase us home every day. Finally one day I said to my brother about one of the boys, "Why are you running? That boy came to school in a stroller."

In those days, the Jewish mothers used to bring their kids to school in big straw strollers. That particular kid would come out of school with us and would be waiting for his mother to arrive with the stroller to take him back home. So one day we just stopped running. And I said to my brother, "Hit him!"

My brother turned around and hit him. And that boy and the others stopped bothering us. But it didn't mean they became friendly. That was a school where they wouldn't even hold our hands playing ring-around-the-rosie and dancing around the maypole. The teachers wouldn't make the kids hold hands either.

I used to beg my mother to move, but my grandfather, Eddie Jones, was a super at 1324 Grant Avenue, and my parents had moved in with him until they could find a place of their own.

After a few years my parents found an apartment and moved to Tinton Avenue and 163rd Street. But the nightmare didn't end there. My grandfather had a relationship with a Miss Bobby, a white lady who lived in the neighborhood, and a lot of people didn't approve. One day after we'd moved to Tinton Avenue, my mother went back to Grant Avenue to see my grandfather and found his body on a radiator, and it was naked and burned. I don't remember if it was ever in the papers because I was just a little girl at the time. But my mother was so shaken up that she denounced God right then and there.

When we moved to Tinton Avenue, I went to P.S. 23, across the street from where they would build the projects, Forest Houses. I loved that school. It was integrated and a very friendly place. We had all kinds of friends—Irish, Italian, Jewish. We didn't think about race there.

It was also a multiracial neighborhood, and our block was a great place to grow up. We played all kinds of games—ringolevio, potsie, skully, that game you played on the street with the bottle caps. And on Saturday morning we'd go and fish in the Crotona Park Lake. You'd take a safety pin and a piece of string, they'd stock the lake with fish for us to catch, and you'd come home with your treasure—a goldfish, right? That was big fun.

My junior high school, J.H.S. 10, didn't have a music program, but my high school, Morris High School, did, and all of us were in the band or the orchestra. I was in the orchestra and played the cello, and the school let me take the cello home so I could practice.

My friend Gene Rudd played the flute. My friend Gary played the bass. And Johnnie Johnson, who's a member of the church I belong to, the Community Church of Morrisania, played drums and guitar and sang.

There were talent shows at Morris all the time. Gene was class singer. Johnnie was class singer. I was class actress. There was also a great theater program at Morris.

It was at Morris where I began everything. Up until then I was really a problem child. I didn't know my own identity; I'd cry if you looked at me for too long. At Morris High School, I became a person. I became alive.

My life at Morris, and before then at P.S. 23 and J.H.S. 10, was very different from my life on Grant Avenue. Once we moved from there, we just didn't have race issues. I'm not saying that there weren't race issues because I remember not being able to eat at White Castle or Howard Johnson's, and they were right here in the Bronx, on Bruckner Boulevard. If you were black, you had to go to the counter and you could do takeout, but you couldn't sit down in the restaurant and eat. That was in the late forties, when Howard Johnson's still had the girls on roller skates serving food. I don't think that changed until the fifties.

When I first went to high school, I played hooky, and a lot. We even had hooky clubs. In junior high school your parents have more control of you, but you had more freedom in high school, changing classes, running, playing in the halls. My father was a chef at the Dixie Kitchen, a soul food place downtown on East Forty-Eighth Street, but my mother, who didn't work, was home all day.

We couldn't play hooky and stay home, right? But there were a couple of students whose mothers did go to work, and we'd play hooky and go to one of those houses. We'd sit around and sing and make up songs, things like that. Teachers would send home cards where you had to say you were absent, and I'd go to the mailbox, open the envelope with a knife, pull the card out, and sign it.

We weren't really doing wild things, not in my first year of high school. But later we'd take the train to high schools in Brooklyn to see the boys, and when we started doing things like that, a lot of the kids who were in my class began to drop out or fail and get left back.

But Morris had great teachers that got you in line. I'll never forget one of them, Lillian Walker. Actually, she wasn't a teacher. She worked in the office, and she took an interest in me. It was because of her that I became interested in my classes and doing well and getting good grades.

It happened this way. One day, when I'd been beginning to fail my classes, Miss Walker came up to me and said, "Something's wrong here. You can't get a good job with this kind of record. I was looking at your record, and you know what I'm going to do? I'm going to take away all of this bad stuff, I want you to start fresh."

She took me under her wing. She taught me how to run the switchboard, and she let me come after school and run it. She taught me office skills. And that changed my life.

Miss Walker wasn't the only one who helped me. One day Jean Martin, my best friend in high school, took me home to meet her aunt Hattie Jackman. I used to go and talk to Hattie at the Trinity Bar and Grill at Teasdale Place and Boston Road, where she worked. I didn't drink. I'd just sit in the bar and talk to her. I imagine my mother wouldn't have been too pleased if she knew I was spending time at a bar, but it had a positive influence on me. Hattie became my mentor, and she's still my best friend today.

I don't know what I would have done without her. I don't know what I would have done without Lillian Walker. And then there was Mr. Miller, the orchestra teacher. If I didn't want to go to a class because I was disturbed about something, he just let me sit in his office and practice. And that's how I got through high school.

Jacqueline Smith Bonneau

Jacqueline Smith Bonneau (1938–) is an educator and jazz pianist.

My family moved from Harlem to Home Street in the Bronx some-time in the early forties. I don't know how they found out about the Bronx—I wasn't even five when they moved there—but even though I was a little girl, I knew this was a better place to live.

My mother was born in New York and my father in St. Augustine, Florida. He had aunts and cousins in St. Augustine and Jacksonville, and I wish I'd gone there when I was a child, but I didn't visit Florida until I was seventeen or eighteen.

My father worked as a Pullman porter, and my mother did domestic work. She used to speak of working in Brighton Beach, Brooklyn, which would have been a long subway ride from the Bronx.

When I started kindergarten, we moved to Lyman Place. I don't know how my mother found the apartment, but this was clearly a move to a bigger and nicer place. We lived in a fifth-floor walkup, and we had access to the roof. The building was spotless.

The building was also mixed racially, which was always a plus be-cause it meant that the landlord would keep the heat going and things repaired. And at least in the beginning Lyman Place was a multiracial block. White families owned the vegetable store and the shoe repair shop. Rudy, a strong German fellow who made potato salad and nice cold cuts, owned the grocery store on 169th Street.

My elementary school was P.S. 54, on Intervale Avenue, just a few minutes' walk from Lyman Place. We had a mix of Italian, Jewish, and black children, but most of the teachers were Italian or Jewish. There were no black teachers.

I don't recall any tensions at the school, but my parents used to talk about politics and racism. My father, who went to Alexander Hamilton High School, didn't go to college, but he was wonderful with current events and history, and we thought he was brilliant.

We had family dinners where people talked about current events or what we did in school. We always had to say the grace: "God is good, God is great. By Thy hand must all be fed, give us Lord our daily bread." From time to time we had to sing it in three-part harmony. So music was a big part of our dinner.

I loved music from the time I knew myself. We didn't have a piano, but we had music from the radio or the phonograph all the time. My parents listened to jazz, show tunes, classical, and religious music, so I was exposed to all kinds of music when I was a child. I just loved it all.

And there was music in the street. I could hear it coming from other people's apartments because at that time we felt safe enough to leave our door open. There were people going in and out of each other's apartments at all hours of the day or night.

Was the neighborhood safe? I don't really know. We were told don't go to a certain block because there were tough kids there. And we weren't allowed to hang out in a grocery store down the street.

The block did have a divide, but it was just a line in the sand. My mother let us make friends with the children up the street because they went to school regularly and wanted to make something of themselves. Not to say the children down the street didn't. But they hung out later and they were in the street. You can't be in the street and do your homework. So it was along those lines that my mother made her decision about who we could play with.

I especially remember the Harris family. They had two children, Paula and Stanley, who were what my mother called nice children. We met a lot of other children who went to church and got good grades in school.

We were a religious family. My parents were Seventh-Day Adventists, God-fearing people, and I went to church in Harlem, to the City Tabernacle Seventh Day Adventist Church on 155th Street. As a Seventh-Day Adventist, you weren't allowed to go to movies or dances.

But I did get formal music instruction. When I was eleven or twelve, my mother enrolled me at the Pelham Music Arts Studio. It was quite a wonderful school because they taught whatever your instrument was. They also taught music theory, which was most unusual for a music school.

And my uncle, Clarence Brareton, took me to Harlem for violin instruction every Monday, to a music teacher in the building where he lived. I'd have an hour of study with her, and then he'd bring me back home.

And of course there was my uncle, the jazz pianist and composer Thelonious Monk. When people asked, "When did you meet him?" I'd say, "He was at the house." He wasn't famous in 1938, when I was born. But he was working on becoming well known and getting his music out there, and we always had copies of his records. Always.

The first record of his that I heard was "'Round Midnight," which I heard in 1948 when I was ten. And that had the biggest influence on me.

I could easily say I saw him every day, but I'm going to say once a week. It wasn't like this made me a celebrity on the block, though, having a musician who was reasonably well known visit all the time. He was just Uncle Thelonious coming by. It wasn't like kids came up to me and asked for his autograph or anything like that.

Then there was the jazz pianist Elmo Hope, who lived on Lyman Place, in the middle of the block. We called him Mr. Elmo, and we'd see him and my uncle together. They'd go to Mr. Elmo's apartment and take turns playing the piano. Other musicians from the neighborhood would come by and jam with them, and when I was ten or eleven, they'd let me bang on the piano. They'd sit there and listen and laugh with each other.

I saw my uncle's Town Hall concert in 1959. But my basic exposure to him was through his records and through him playing at Mr. Elmo's house and at his own house on West Sixty-Third Street. I also remember the woman they called the Baroness. When Thelonious brought her to the Bronx, we found out that she was a tremendous advocate for jazz and jazz musicians. She'd take him to the different spots where he was playing. That's how we got to know her as a person.

I remember that she drove a Bentley, and sometimes he'd take us in the car. She'd come through the block with the top down and all of the heads turned. People would say, "Who's that?" Uncle Thelonious was always important to us, but when the Baroness arrived in that car I thought he must be important to the world.

When I was growing up, Lyman Place was idyllic. But then heroin started to come into the neighborhood. In 1953, when I was fifteen, one of my neighbors, Richard Manson, died in his sleep. His mother asked me to come over to her apartment because he wasn't moving. That's when I realized he'd died from an overdose.

I was in high school at the time, and this was something people were talking about. It was a big deal. And when heroin hit Lyman Place, it changed our sense of how safe we were. We lived on the top floor, and a lot of the addicts would go to the roof. We couldn't keep the door open like we used to.

Then we had the experience of my own cousin, who grew up with us. He was like a brother. We lost him when he was twenty-three to an overdose of drugs. I think it was around 1960. So the drug epidemic really hit us hard. By this point, some families were moving away, and at a certain point people were afraid to walk home from the subway at night. Some of the shops were beginning to move away too because they were being hit with robberies, and people were buying more locks. Everybody was on edge.

My uncle Thelonious moved in with us around 1956 because of a fire in his apartment and moved in again in 1961. The first time he stayed about eight months. The second time it was longer, maybe about two years. He was there with his wife and his two children. And he wasn't the only one. My family took in a lot of people over the years.

My father was a real lover of music and musicians, and he was an open-hearted guy. So there was always another place at the table for a musician. And if a family member got into any difficulty or fell on hard times, our home was the home to come to.

We had three bedrooms, and there were nine of us—my mother, my father, and seven children. When we took in Thelonious and his family, that made thirteen. They slept on folding couches, and we made the living room into another bedroom. We didn't have bunk beds, and no one had their own bed except my mother and father. We just doubled up the best we could.

And we finally got a piano. I got a Steinway baby grand piano, which Thelonious picked out. To get it into a five-story walkup, they took the legs off. There was a lot of activity around the piano because we loved music. My father played it a lot. He wasn't a keyboard person; he played the mandolin. But he had a lot of fun on that piano.

As I said, for a while it was idyllic living on Lyman Place. But at a certain point I began to think, "I'm not going to live in this neighborhood all my life." I've got to start thinking about going somewhere else. I got a partial scholarship to Atlantic Union College, a Seventh-Day Adventist college in South Lancaster, Massachusetts. I went in 1958, stayed for a year, then came home and got married in 1960. After I got married, I moved to Brooklyn, but I came back to Lyman Place because my family was still there, and they stayed until 1965.

People ask me about a song Thelonious Monk wrote called "Jackie-ing" that was named after me and dedicated to me. I remember I was at his house on West Sixty-Third Street, and he played something he was writing. He didn't have a title. Then in a spiral notebook he wrote "Jackie-ing." So I have a famous piece of music named after me. I always felt humbled by it.

When I think about the amazing experience of growing up on Lyman Place, the main thing I remember is that Thelonious Monk touched so many lives. I had a very unique childhood, almost unbelievable. The kind of people I came in contact with—I'm in awe of my own life.

Hetty Fox

Hetty Fox (1938–), a former professor at San Fernando Valley State College (now California State University, Northridge), ran a nonprofit community center on Lyman Place in Morrisania.

I was born in Harlem, where I lived on 122nd Street between Seventh and Eighth Avenues. In 1940, my family moved to Prospect Avenue in the Bronx. When we moved there, it was a lovely neighborhood. Trees up and down Prospect Avenue, and I was so thrilled when we turned the corner and my dad pointed to the house two doors down and said, "This is where we are going to live."

At that time I think we were the first black homeowners, and we were definitely the first black family on the block. There was a family called the Muranchis who lived next door. They had twin girls, the same age as I was, who challenged me when they saw me there. They said, "Hey! What are you doing in that house?" I said, "My father had already bought this house." So they said, "Well, you come down here, we'll slap your face!" So I said, "Stay right there!"

Something told me that if I ran from them the first day I was going to be in deep trouble so I backed off. And soon we became friends. We never had a fight, we got sick from eating sandwich cookies in their basement playroom, and they came to my birthday parties. But that was my introduction to the block. I met the challenge, and we went on from there.

We had a lot of stickball games around here. Today I tell children in the neighborhood about the sewer down the street and my brother, who was a three-sewer man. He would hit the ball all the way from there up to the roofs on Freeman Street. When I show them that distance they say that those were giants I'd play with.

I started school at P.S. 54, on Intervale and Freeman Street, and then I went to St. Anthony of Padua over on Prospect and 166th, the school the Chantels came out of. I played basketball there, and I was the foul-shooting champion of the Bronx and New York City. After St. Anthony's I went to Cathedral High School in Manhattan and then to Hunter College.

I never remember feeling unsafe, even coming home at ten or eleven at night. I could get off the subway at midnight and have no qualms. In fact, when I was at Hunter and going to night school, quite often I came home at eleven at night, and I never felt unsafe. I don't know whether it was because of ignorance or what, but I felt the comfort in my neighborhood. I always walked with purpose. I didn't wander around aimlessly. I was working at the public library in the science and technology stocking division, and my mind was occupied.

When I was growing up, there were a lot of stores within walking distance. Southern Boulevard was always a good shopping area. The Boston Road area had many more stores than it does now, although they haven't done too badly considering the slaughtering we saw here. My father was a tailor who used to run a factory downtown, and my mother used to sew. She taught me to knit and sew when I was four years old, and we used to walk to Bathgate Avenue to get buttons and string.

Southern Boulevard down by Freeman was also filled with stores. Wilkins Avenue, which is now called Louis Nine Boulevard, was full of hardware stores, clothing stores, things like that. There was also a Woolworth's there, where I worked when I was growing up. I think I told a fib about my age to get the job, but anyway, I worked there and earned some money for school.

We also went to Crotona Park. I've been going to Crotona Park since I was sixteen, and I learned to swim in the pool. I also went to Ninety-Nine Park, which is not too far from here. Ninety-Nine Park became very famous for hip-hop, but back in the fifties and sixties it was also famous for basketball. My brother, George Fox, played for St. Anthony's, for Cardinal Hayes High School, and for St. Francis College in Brooklyn, and so he was good friends with people like Floyd Lane of City College. And that's how I learned to play.

I used to have to go get my brother at Ninety-Nine Park and bring him home. Then I played basketball on their courts. They used to send my brother to come get me, and then my mother had to send my little sister to get both of us, because if I was playing basketball, my brother used to bet on me to shoot from half court. I had a hook shot.

Even back then there were signs of change. Back in the forties and early fifties the neighborhood had been so safe that we used to sleep with our doors open. We used to sleep on the fire escape. We didn't lock our doors or anything. Then all of a sudden around the late fifties we noticed young men sneaking around, climbing into apartments through windows, and we said, "What the heck is wrong with that guy?"

At first the changes didn't seem so ominous. We presumed that someone in the city would be taking charge and doing something. But it didn't happen. And then things just escalated.

I had moved to California in 1964 to take part in the free speech movement, and the next thing I knew I decided to stay a little bit longer. I started working at the California Department of Employment, working on unemployment insurance, and then I went into vocational counseling and became a job specialist. I specialized in the skilled trades—engine lathe operators, machinists—working with a lot of guys out of San Fernando Valley.

I was living in Hollywood. In 1965, after the riots in Watts, they opened up four or five new training centers, and I was head counselor of one of those centers. Then I took a job teaching psychology, sociology, and race relations at Cal State Northridge.

A person might ask why anyone would leave being a professor. I liked to say I've been a professor since I was three. But I never think you should place your profession on a higher level than your humanness and your home. In my opinion, you should be bringing your talents and skills to your home, to your family. That's the highest calling, not the titles and the degrees.

In 1970 I decided to come home. My sister was expecting a baby, and she and her husband were planning to move to Brazil. I wanted to see her before she left. So when I came home to say goodbye to her, I returned to Lyman Place and saw the creeping signs of deterioration.

When I saw the conditions, I didn't know what I was going to do. And of course, being older, I knew that it was extremely dangerous that so many houses were being consumed by fire. It was like an angel of death, with a sword, moving from Vyse Avenue and slowly creeping up the hill. Not in a million years could I have imagined what would happen to the neighborhood where I grew up. It was the shock of that change that got me moving.

Somehow we were able to stop the deterioration at Stebbins Avenue, which is now called the Rev. James A. Polite Avenue. And the singer Maxine Sullivan, God rest her soul, who used to have a place called the House of Jazz on Stebbins right near me, was also fighting to stop the deterioration from going any farther. So somehow we managed to kind of keep this little village relatively unscathed. I didn't know what was happening on the other streets. I just knew I was trying to keep Lyman Place intact.

At the time we didn't realize how devastating these initial signs were of what was to come. The feeling was that people were just moving away. There was a huge turnover in population between the sixties and the seventies. People had stopped caring, and the city wasn't taking care of abandoned properties. Buildings were being emptied out, but it just looked like normal erosion.

Even so, I knew immediately that this was a very serious problem because it was unconscionable to think that buildings would stay empty for so long. I remember one day when I [went] downtown, and when I got home a building that had been there when I left was gone. I had never seen something like that in my life.

You don't think that a neighborhood will change so fast. You don't think that the population of a neighborhood will change so fast. You think you're going to be able to come home and talk to people you know. So when you come home and find that nobody recognizes you, you're thinking, "Where's so and so?" And you're thinking, "Well, something has changed."

When I came back in 1970, I was going to write a book about some of the things I'd learned in California. This is when the whole surge of black studies was just beginning, with people like Angela Davis and Maulana Karenga. So there was an emerging sense of people coming together to try to make a meaningful difference in their neighborhood.

When I came home I was going to pursue work related to what I had learned during the sixties, and I was going to do it in my father's basement. Then I came out one day and realized that there were problems in the buildings on my block. So I thought, well, whatever work I was doing wouldn't mean anything if the buildings were destroyed, so I said I better start saving houses.

I began going to community meetings. The city had given dispossess notices to people in two of the main buildings on the street. The building next door was already empty, and so was the one across the street. I thought this was outrageous. This was a danger to the children. That's when I began to do something.

My first step was to save the house on the corner, right next door to my dad's house. I created an afterschool program for children there, and that went on for about fifteen years. We stayed open six nights a week until 10:30. We had chess, we had checkers. I put up my list of 186 African tribes. I put up words from eleven African languages. I taught them African styles of dance.

I was dancing at the time. I was performing with a group from Swaziland in southern Africa, and we did performances up and down the East Coast. I had danced on the West Coast with an African dance ensemble. On weekends we'd perform at places like UC Santa Barbara and UCLA, and then I'd do my teaching during the week. I still have my drums. That's always an integral part of the music and the dance.

I was aware of hip-hop when it started because we had the corner building, and we used to have a DJ stand where kids would train to DJ for parties. So I'd try to make available to them the electricity or a small stage in the storefront so kids could get their act together.

When the burning of this part of the Bronx took place, it was almost impossible to get people and businesses to invest in the area. The destruction was so devastating and so continuous that businesses just wanted to flee.

I held four international energy conferences on this block. For the fourth one I invited people from thirty-nine countries. On the front of the flyer that I made, I listed the names of all the countries represented. On the back I put a map of the restaurants that still existed, that came through the horror—one on Boston Road and eleven others in the area. There's one on Southern Boulevard that's still there.

The reason I put the names of the restaurants on the flyer was to answer the questions that people from other countries had about coming to the South Bronx: Are people still alive there? Can we get something to eat there? Can we go to the bathroom? I figured these maps would answer those questions so we wouldn't have to say, "Yes, you can come here. We're still alive."

Still, what was happening to the areas was shocking and frightening. Mayor Koch, who put Neighborhood Preservation Offices in many places around the city, would not put an office in this area. He said we were too far gone. To me this meant we were totally vulnerable. If we were the most devastated area in the country—that is, having the most abandoned housing—without there having been a war, and we were also the poorest part of the country, that seemed to me a pretty clear indication of where we stood.

If your body gets cut, everyone rushes over to figure out what happened, what went wrong. And they try to start healing those wounds. We had the biggest cut in U.S. history here, and no one came. They just looked at what was happening as though they were watching television.

I think that because of the desire to get out of the neighborhood, people who lived here never had a tight, cohesive response. Of course some people tried to help. They tried to save buildings that were going to be abandoned. But though they could get rid of the guys who were doing the vandalism, they couldn't get the city to respond quickly and stop the devastation.

There was a constant erosion of people who had the wherewithal and the brainpower and the passion to attack these problems but who didn't stick it out. Even the leaders and mentors eventually left. We once had a spirit about our neighborhood, about our blocks, but that spirit wasn't put into action when the fires hit.

The whole idea of defending home base is integral to everybody in the world. And so I had to devise so many strategies just to make people feel at home here, to make sure mothers would feel comfortable. Because if a mother doesn't feel comfortable, she's not going to correct her children. She's not going to say don't break the windows, don't do this, don't do that. My feeling was, I had to focus on the buildings and make sure that mothers felt comfortable.

Remember they used to have night centers? That's what prompted me to have the building on the corner stay open till ten-thirty every night, six nights a week, because I remembered the night centers. With night centers, at least kids knew they had some place to go.

When I was growing up most of the families were two-parent families where the father was working, but at a certain point that mold cracked apart. There are absolutely no adult male influences to speak of.

I try to emphasize family, like with the lanyards I give out every day. Everyone gets a lanyard of two colors. But guys with eight children can get lanyards with three colors, so a lot of times guys will come up and say, well, I want three colors. And I say, how many children do you have? And they say, I don't have any children. I'm not married. So I say, well, when you get married and have eight kids you can have three colors because we value family life very much.

There's one family on the block where the mother had eight children. And those eight children were born right here on Lyman. The mother was born on Lyman, and the father, who was originally from the South, grew up on Lyman.

The whole purpose of fighting to save the building was to try to preserve family life. We wanted to save the buildings so they could help maintain family life and encourage children to understand relationships. And this is like the third set of kids I've been raising.

But there's still a tendency for kids to move away. I've lost some beautiful kids who lived on this block, fabulous beautiful young women. I remember growing up, we had gorgeous women. My brother was madly in love with Juanita across the street, and Charlene, and so on. Where did those gorgeous women go? They should be here. Love, beauty, music, dance—whatever we can use to help to persuade people to understand the values in New York; the real struggle is sticking together.

I realized from early on that I couldn't approach this project as an academic issue. I had to build on the feelings I had growing up here on Lyman Place. So I began to apply those principles and use my academic background to help bolster that.

But basically you have to be there. You have to live there, and you have to demonstrate your care by what you do. You have to presume you're on camera at all times because there's always a three-year-old in the window watching you, a child who may not speak English, but she knows what you're doing with a broom. You're sweeping the street. You're out there demonstrating that. Or you're turning on the hydrant, or you're making little things for children, or you're helping adults. Every year we have a Christmas party for a hundred kids. My Christmas tree is still up—as much of a tree as we have—but that was a celebration anyway.

You also have to create events and annual things that children can look forward to, that the neighborhood can look forward to. I read three newspapers a day, and the children know it, and they know I do a radio show—again I'm demonstrating by what I do—so they're absorbing all this, and hopefully they'll make use of some of it in their future.

I want their bag of tricks to be big. I want them to have a wide variety of things they can recall and remember. That's why the list of tribes and languages is on the wall. Every now and then they might look up on the wall and see those things.

Every summer we go to Bear Mountain State Park in upstate New York. We just had our Bear Mountain trip last week, and we got back just as the blackout hit. So the blackout was like one big party for us. People were dragging everything out of their refrigerator and cooking it up the sidewalk. The party lasted all through the night.

When we had the blackout of '77, I dragged out my drums, and I got on the subway and went over to Prospect Avenue, and we were playing. The cops were there, trying to stop all the vandals, and they heard this sound, so they swooped up with their lights on, and they realized pretty quickly that we were just playing music, and they looked shocked. They didn't know what to do. So they just rode off, and we just kept on playing.

James Pruitt

James Pruitt (1938–) was a long-time social studies teacher and department chair at Morris and Kennedy High Schools.

My family moved to the Bronx from Harlem in, I think, 1932. I base that on the fact that my oldest sister said she attended elementary school in Manhattan but moved to the Bronx and went to P.S. 23, which was at 165th Street between Union and Tinton Avenue. The family first lived on Prospect Avenue, then moved to 818 166th Street, next to St. Anthony's Roman Catholic Church. I was born in that building.

My father was from Alabama, my mother was from South Carolina, and they met in Harlem in the 1920s. My father was a World War I vet, and he'd come to New York after the war looking for work. He chose New York because his brother was already here and was living in Harlem.

My parents met through my uncle Bob, who was taking a course in prosthetic dentistry at the Harlem YMCA along with my dad. Bob had a large apartment on West 129th Street, and when his sisters came to New York, they decided to live with him. But Bob didn't want the responsibility of taking care of his sisters, so he decided he would marry them off. He met these two gentlemen in the class who seemed like they were responsible and introduced them to his sisters. That's how my dad and mom got together and later my aunt and uncle got together.

After my parents were married, they lived in Harlem for a short pe-

riod of time, and then they moved to the Bronx. I imagine they decided
on the Bronx through association with people in their church because
the Harlem churches were like magnets for people from certain communities. The church we grew up in, Grace Congregational Church of
Harlem on 139th Street, had a membership that was largely Southern.
But within the church there were auxiliaries. There was the South Carolina Club, and other clubs made of people from Georgia and Alabama.
There were also a few people from the West Indies, some from Ber-
muda and Guyana.

In Harlem, my family lived on Bradhurst Avenue, a street that runs
alongside Colonial Park, which is down the hill from Sugar Hill. A lot
of people who lived in that community moved to the Bronx. I could
name family after family.

I don't think my parents moved to get better housing. I suspect it
was a question of money. This was the Depression, and it might have
been cheaper to move to the Bronx. Subways and trolleys were five
cents, so transportation back to Manhattan was relatively cheap. And
there were transfers, so you could come from the Bronx, take a bus or a
trolley, and transfer to another one, all for five cents one way.

When my parents moved to the Bronx, my father worked in the post
office, and he was also a clothes presser at a local cleaning establish-
ment at Prospect Avenue and Home Street owned by a guy named Joe
Siciliano. That was convenient because my family was living across the
street, on Prospect Avenue between Home Street and 168th Street.

It was a changing neighborhood—largely Jewish with a few blacks
moving in. Most of the black men who were heads of households
worked for the post office. I could probably name fifteen families where
the fathers worked for the post office. I was told by a colleague whose
father was a rental agent named Mr. Klein that he only rented to black
families if the husband or father worked for the post office because the
agent could always get his rent if they came up short. He could get the
rent from the government.

Sociologically it was fascinating because at four o'clock all these men
came up the street from the subways and buses and headed home with
newspapers under their arms. They were all wearing gray uniforms, and
they were all tired.

My mother was a full-time homemaker when her children were
young. She had a college education, but in those days men were proud

to say, "My wife raises our family and provides for the home, and I provide for the family." My father didn't want my mother to work, so she didn't work until he retired. But then she said, "I'm not staying home with you," and she got a full-time job.

Even after my family left Harlem, they continued to attend Grace Congregational Church. Harlem remained the social and cultural center even for those black families who had moved to the Bronx. The churches were in Harlem, and so were all the entertainment centers. So even if a family lived in the Bronx, most of these families would return to Harlem on Sunday morning to go to church.

I don't think the Bronx ever became a cultural center for black people the way Harlem did. But politically, people identified with the Bronx, and they supported candidates for political office from the neighborhood, like Councilman Wendell Foster. The political activity developed from various neighborhood organizations and civic groups started by the women who lived in that community.

There was one organization called the Exclusive 9—the EX9—that used to raise money for various civic groups. And we had a block association that gave a tea once a year, and all the money from the tea went to scholarships to send kids to camp.

The one church in the community that did make a big impression was St. Augustine's Presbyterian Church on 165th Street and Prospect Avenue. In the 1930s, it was largely a white church and not so fast to change. But I'm told that a woman by the name of Angie Dickerson, who was a member of the congregation, persuaded the church to bring in a black minister. A man named Edler Hawkins, a very low-key yet dynamic minister, was assigned to the church, and he attracted a large number of families.

So people now had a choice. They could go to church in their own community or they could return to Harlem. A lot of people opted to go back to Harlem, but others went to St. Augustine's, which had a number of activities after church and during the week.

My Cub Scout group was located there, a group of teenagers met in the church house on Sundays, and a number of other organizations were located there. The New York City Mission Society had leadership programs there, and there was a cadet program that met at that church. They had a basketball court in the basement and a basketball team called the Knights. St. Augustine's was a significant cultural organization, and anybody who lived in that area during the thirties, forties, and fifties would identify strongly with that church.

We were homeowners; the bank and our family owned our home. But most of my sisters' friends, who were older than me, lived in apartments or even in small houses. We were, I think, unique in that we had our own home, but my parents wouldn't have been able to afford to buy the house if it hadn't been for the generosity of a doctor who lived next door. When the house came up for sale, the doctor cosigned for the mortgage because he wanted to choose his neighbors. He knew our family, and he knew that there were five kids.

I went to P.S. 99, which is on Stebbins Avenue between Home Street and 167th Street. My brother, Henry, who is four years older, also attended that school. My sisters attended P.S. 54, which is on Intervale Avenue.

The neighborhood was a strong, middle-income area. On my block alone there were two doctors. Some of the older children who lived next door to me were social workers or nurses, and some of the dads worked in the post office. So families owned homes, and they took care of their homes.

The lady next door to us on the other side, Mrs. Stripper, belonged to St. Augustine's, and once a year her auxiliary would give a dinner— I can still smell the baked bread and the fried chicken. The people of the church would come to her backyard; my parents would roll back the fence between our yard and hers so people could expand into our yard, and both yards would be lit up.

There was a lot of sharing, a lot of nurturing. Not everyone had a car, of course. Our family didn't. But when we went away to summer camp, our neighbors would drive our family up on visiting day to see us.

When the doctor who lived next door to us bought a country home in Dutchess County, he'd take me and my brother up to spend time there because it was a big beautiful mansion with a lot of yard for us to run around in. He also had an office next door to our home, and when he visited patients, which doctors did in those days, he'd take us in the car, and we'd sit there and wait for him. And he had some nice cars, Cadillacs and Packards.

The first housing project in my community was the Forest Houses, which were under construction in the mid-fifties when I was a student at Morris High School. I remember every brick that was laid. But that didn't change my perception of where I grew up, which I saw as a middle-class area. Not that everyone was middle class, but I don't remember class distinctions. My best friend lived across the street from me in the basement of an apartment building where his father was the janitor, and we're still friends today.

There were tough blocks nearby, though. You'd go around the corner to Union Avenue, and you might have your head handed to you. There definitely were some tough kids. But because the neighborhood was stable, and it was very seldom that people moved in or out, you had a certain protection. Everybody knew everybody, so if Curtis beat you up, and everybody knew Curtis, your parents would go to Curtis's family to complain, and that might put an end to it.

There was a live-and-let-live attitude. I don't remember the police being called for anything. Everybody knew who the good kids were, or the soft kids, and they left them alone. And the tough kids you didn't mess with.

Achievement was measured by your athletic ability. If you were on the football team or the basketball team at your school, you were one of the gods. But people were also recognized for their academic achievements. If you could get into someplace like Bronx High School of Science, that was something to be appreciated, not be put down for. Getting good grades at school was valued, and so was getting into what became the City University.

My parents shopped at Safeway and the A&P. Safeway was at the corner of Boston Road next to what became Sylvia's Blue Morocco, and the A&P was at McGinley Square. One was five blocks away; the other was six blocks away. One of the jobs my brother and I did was we'd get a cart or wagon, and we'd help ladies home with their groceries. Which meant standing outside of the store and saying, "Ma'am, can I help you with your groceries?" We'd take the groceries home with them, pulling the cart as the person walked along the streets, and then we'd find out that the ladies lived on the top floor and they had sixteen bags of groceries. And you'd take the bags upstairs, and she'd give you twenty cents. But it was a way for us to have a little pocket change.

Mrs. Keel owned the corner candy store. She had a big jar of pickles on the counter, along with jars of pigs' ears and pigs' feet. She sold all kinds of candy and was known as an informal source of neighborhood news—who was sleeping with who, what kid got shot, things like that. I think she was German.

Along with the youth activities at St. Augustine's there were other youth activities when I was growing up. Once the housing projects opened up, they all had community centers. There was also PAL—the Police Athletic League—and the New York City Mission Society, which had leadership training programs in a lot of the churches in the South Bronx. Then there was Forest House, on Forest Avenue near Morris High School, which was a cross between a settlement house and a community center. They gave music lessons and taught art classes, things like that.

I took music lessons in my home from a young man named Harold Brown who lived down the block. For one thing, we had a piano, and if you had a piano you had an advantage. Harold Brown was one of seven children in a family where everyone was musical. They lived down the street from us, and our parents were friends. I loved to go to the Browns' apartment because they had two pianos. You'd go there and see the family eating breakfast around the kitchen table, and in the living room and the dining room were these huge pianos. One was an upright piano, and the other was a grand piano.

My introduction to elementary school came when I was about four. My mother was a volunteer at P.S. 40. P.S. 40 eventually became Prospect Junior High School, but in those days it was a first-through-eighth-grade school. During World War II, they needed volunteers in case of an air-raid attack. So my mother went to the school, and she'd help the teachers, serving as what today would be called a school aide. In exchange for her service I got to sit in the kindergarten room. I was younger than the other kids, but I got to have the milk and cookies along with them.

When I was old enough for school I went to P.S. 99. In the first and second grade all the teachers were white and mostly Jewish. In the third grade I had a woman whose name was Mrs. Lady, and I thought she was the oldest woman in the world. She was kind of heavyset and slow moving, and she was very strict.

Each day the class would take a trip to the bathroom. Everyone would have to line up according to height, and the class would march down the hall to the bathrooms. On one occasion, we were headed back to our room, and I was the next-to-the-last boy in the line because I was tall. For some reason she was reprimanding the boy behind me, and I shuddered. She thought I was laughing, and she smacked me.

It was a Friday, so I went home and told my parents about it. Mrs. Lady didn't appear on Monday, and on Tuesday we were told that she had passed away. Needless to say, there wasn't a lot of sympathy for her.

Mrs. Lady was replaced by a black woman named Lodi Smith, a substitute who lived on Lyman Place, two blocks from the school. Lodi Smith had a daughter who was the same age as all the kids in the class. The daughter went to parochial school, but after school she'd stop by and pick up her mom so they could go home together, so we'd always see her. And when the daughter had a birthday the whole class was invited to Mrs. Smith's home. This was nice because it was like a social thing with a teacher in the neighborhood. I thought Mrs. Smith was just wonderful. She owned the candy store on 167th Street, which was at the other end of the school block, and her husband ran the store during the day when his wife was at school.

Mrs. Smith was replaced by another black woman named Inez Singletary, who was a classmate of one of my older sisters at Hunter College. This was also wonderful. Now I had a teacher who not only knew my family but was young and active and very concerned about the kids and our learning process. I felt very special.

I didn't see much racial tension growing up. If people didn't like blacks, they just moved away. More black and Latino families were coming to the community, but it was apparent to me that the community was divided racially in terms of where people lived. The white people lived on one side of P.S. 99, and the black people lived on the other side. So the schoolyard was like a meeting place for all of the groups.

But there were some neighborhoods in the Bronx I was afraid to go to. If you took the bus from where I lived on Prospect Avenue and you came to Fordham Plaza, the bus would pass through 188th Street, which was the Belmont section, the Italian section. If you got off the bus before it got to Fordham Plaza, you might get beat up. That was the threat.

So you couldn't get off the bus in Belmont. And people used to report incidents of residents of that community throwing things at the bus if they saw black faces. I don't know if that's true, but it was considered a closed community. We weren't welcomed there, so we didn't go there.

But we weren't afraid of the housing projects. They were an opportunity for people to get decent housing. I wasn't aware that they had problems until much later. When my wife was growing up, she had great times with her cousins, who lived in the Harlem River Houses. The Harlem River Houses are one of America's oldest public housing projects, and the people who lived there were so proud of living in a decent place that it was well maintained and it was kind of an ideal setting.

Because of the success of that project, other projects were built. Except that the decision makers decided that if a few people could live in places like the Harlem River Houses, why not build bigger Harlem River Houses all over? And that was a mistake because they put too many people in the same place, they didn't set the same standards, and there were no penalties for abusing the property.

So you had people living there who didn't know how to take care of elevators that might go up to the twelfth or twentieth or twenty-fifth floor, and if they weren't working people would have to walk. People would also airmail their garbage out the window instead of putting it in the appropriate places. And when you had a lot of low-income families living in the same space and the children were unsupervised or there were no supervised activities for them after school, that was a problem too.

But when they first built the Forest Houses, which was at Tinton Avenue at 163rd Street, my family saw the project as something positive because along with the housing project they put in a nursery and a community center. So it brought facilities to a community that didn't have those sorts of things. And everything was available not only to the people who lived in the Forest Houses but also to the people who lived in the area.

White flight in Morrisania began to be visible right after World War II. But one neighborhood institution that remained integrated all through the 1950s was Morris High School. Morris was one of the most wonderful high schools in the city. They had an academic curriculum, they had a commercial curriculum, and they had a general curriculum.

I'm a retired teacher, but comparing myself to the teachers I had there, I had some of the most skilled individuals that I've ever seen anywhere. The reason I taught social studies was because my high school social studies teachers were all terrific.

A few teachers stand out. I remember a guy named Lenny Littman, who was a World War II vet. He later became principal of Stevenson High School, and he always brought his experiences into the classroom. I also remember a woman named Joy Schrizer, who was, I think, my social studies teacher in the tenth grade. She went on to become a social studies teacher at John F. Kennedy High School. I became her colleague, and I'm still friendly with her today.

The school was very integrated, and every group was represented. I also remember white kids coming to visit me. We had a house, and most of my classmates didn't. So I had white kids over to my house. I mean I had a yard—come on. So we'd go to my house after school, and we cooked some mickeys—potatoes—in the backyard. It wasn't unusual for me to have Larry Colombo and Barry Kahn and Stanley Channersman come to my house. And I'd go to their house because they had televisions and I didn't. It wasn't an everyday kind of thing, but it happened during the first three or four grades of school.

After I graduated from Morris High School, I went to Lincoln University in Pennsylvania, which is America's oldest historically black college.

In the Bronx in the 1950s and 1960s, the opportunity to go to college was there, but a lot of families couldn't afford it. Hunter College and City College and perhaps Brooklyn and Queens were free, but to get in you had to have a decent average. So your average, which usually had to be over 85, and an entrance exam would determine whether you got into the college of your choice. If that didn't happen, your parents would have to pay for you to go to college.

My four siblings were smart enough to go to Hunter College for free. However, I didn't earn that kind of an average. I think part of the reason was that I wasn't a serious student in high school. I did lots of activities. I was in the Order of the Feather fraternity. I was in the choir; I was in the leadership training program. So for students like me, whose parents had to pay for them to go to college because they didn't get into the city universities, black colleges were less expensive than local colleges.

I didn't go directly to college after high school. I went to Hunter in the evening, but that was a general-studies program. Then one day my mom said to me, "when are you going to college?" I knew someone who was a Lincoln alumni, and he wrote a letter of recommendation for me. I went to Lincoln from 1960 to 1964, and I think I had the richest college experience of all of my siblings, partly because I lived on campus. I was at a university that was financially struggling, but it had a rich curriculum. I was president of my class, I was business manager of the glee club, I worked in the alumni office. And I made friends.

In the sixties, one-third of the students were from Africa, another third were from Pennsylvania, and the others were from the rest of the country. The brother of Nnamdi Azikiwe, the first president of Nigeria, was one of my classmates. Some of the students became quite promi-

nent in their own fields. We got a really solid education, and after graduation maybe five of us became teachers and the rest went to law school
and medical school and became rich.

I had avoided becoming a teacher because my sisters and my brother
were teachers, and my mom had trained to be a teacher. My secret desire was to be a television news broadcaster. They didn't have any black
television news broadcasters back then, but that was something I was
interested in.

Ed Bradley of the TV show *60 Minutes* had gone to Cheney State
College, which was just down the road from me, at the same time I
was in college. He followed his dream. I didn't. I took the safe route
and went to the classroom, which was something I knew how to do. I
knew I'd be comfortable with teaching, and I knew people who did it,
and I knew what the risks were. I was fortunate enough to get my first
teaching job from the school I graduated from, which was Morris High
School.

My first encounters with racism came when I started teaching at
Morris in 1964. I was the new kid on the block, and I had a few issues
with my fellow teachers. First, one of the younger teachers who wasn't
accustomed to seeing black teachers, especially black male teachers,
assumed that I was an aide and made disparaging remarks about me just
out of earshot. One of my peers informed the woman, who turned all
kinds of shades of red, that I was not an aide and that I was also not the
elevator operator. I was a teacher and should be treated with respect.

Then there was an incident involving my chairman. I ate lunch every
day with two black nurses who worked in the school. Apparently there
was some discussion among the senior faculty about the black people
eating together. And so my chairman came to me and asked me if I'd
join him for lunch. I said the union contract was my own and I could
eat with whomever I want to eat with. Not that I had anything against
him, but I valued the relationship I had with these two women, and I
chose to eat with them. When he told me he was concerned that all
the black people were eating together, I reminded him that the white
people were doing the same thing. So there were all kinds of ways to
look at segregation.

I was the first teacher at Morris to teach Negro history. I wrote the
curriculum, which I probably have a copy of somewhere. The way the
course came about was like this. I had a club called the African American Culture Club. And once I had a group of students who were inter-

ested in finding out more about the subject, we went to the principal, and I said there was all this interest in the subject and the kids in the club would like to have a course in it.

Having graduated from Lincoln, where I was a history major, I'd taken all these courses, not only traditional courses but also black history courses. Lincoln had a black history curriculum, they had an African history curriculum, and they had an African politics curriculum. I must have had forty or more credits in various history courses, plus I had professors who had lived through a lot of those experiences. So I was ready to teach black history.

I'd learned about Negro history, black history, African American history, whatever you want to call it, through my parents and through the personal experiences of people we knew. But my first formal introduction to it was in courses I took at Lincoln University, and that's what I drew upon when I developed my course at Morris.

Paul Himmelstein

Paul Himmelstein (1941–), who at the age of twelve became the lead singer of the Heartbreakers, a doo-wop group, works as a doorman in Manhattan.

I was the eleventh of fourteen children, and when I was little I lived on Jennings Street at Prospect Avenue in Morrisania. There were a few big families, and we were one of them. There was the Chandler family—they had seventeen—and the Browns had ten. The Elis family had nine. I really thought I was born there, but when I had to get a birth certificate for school, I noticed that I was born on Bathgate Avenue. My family moved probably because they needed a bigger place, and the one we moved to had six rooms.

My father worked seven days a week. During the week [he] drove a truck delivering live poultry, and on weekends he drove a cab. Then he hurt his wrist and couldn't lift those crates.

Both my parents were Jewish, and they both spoke Yiddish. They used to speak Yiddish when they had little arguments over stupid things around the house, and I learned a few Jewish words that way.

My earliest memories of the neighborhood, from when I was three or four years old, were that your mother could sit on the stoop late on summer nights while you played in front of the building with your friends. I remember my sister buying me a rocking horse; I never forgot that. There was a shoemaker who had little toys in the corner of his building. It was the kind of neighborhood where you played stickball and street games with chalk on the sidewalk. Sometime you had a one neighborhood playing against another neighborhood.

I never really got into that because I guess I wasn't sporty enough. I never got picked. Once or twice I did because they were short-handed, so they had no choice but to take me. They needed another guy for second base or something.

It was the kind of neighborhood where you made scooters from a skate. You took a board, put the skate on it with a nail, and put a milk crate on top. These were the kinds of toys we had.

On Halloween, you went trick-or-treating to the Wilkins Avenue Market, a Jewish market on Wilkins and Jennings Street. Near that market was a five-and-ten-cents store, Jewish delis, and restaurants. My mother used to shop there.

When we got home from school, the door was always unlocked. Nobody locked their doors. You just walked in. Many times I went home, nobody was in the house, and I'd be calling for my mother. She might have been at a neighbor's house or watching soap operas on TV.

We were one of the first people on our block to get a TV. My father hit the number; I think he won five hundred dollars. The next thing we know, one day they delivered this three-way combination TV, record player, and radio. I'll tell you the truth, it was like going to the movies in your house. I remember sitting around the radio in my house. You made it your business to get upstairs because *The Shadow* was coming on. You sat around the radio listening to these dramas and eating potato chips.

This was just after World War II. I remember the sirens going off and everybody had to shut their lights off. My father went out on the street because he was an air-raid warden. I knew that because once I looked out the window and he was standing in the gutter pointing at people and saying, "Shut off your lights. Shut off your lights."

By the time I was five or six, it was a mostly black neighborhood. All my friends in my age bracket were black. The super was black. But there were also Spanish. Our block was mostly black, but Freeman Street near Wilkins Avenue, where the Jewish market was, became mostly Spanish as I got older. The white people became fewer and fewer.

I'll be honest with you. I didn't pay much attention to the fact that white people were moving away from the neighborhood. I knew there were white people in the next building. When I was a little kid, like two or three years old, I'd hear my sisters calling out the backyard window to their girlfriends, who were white. There were white people still living in the next building. But when I went into the street as a little boy, my mother was out there sitting on the stoop with other neighbors, and they were black. So the neighborhood was becoming predominantly more black, but there were still whites around. I just didn't pay attention because you're just a little boy and you're not watching things like that.

Back then they used to have the rag man, who came around and collected rags and sang. He'd sing in the backyards, and you'd throw money down. You'd hear a voice singing, and you opened up the window. I don't remember how it got discovered that I could sing. My brother Larry, who was a year older than me, he was known as the singer in the family. People used to knock on our door and say, "Call your brother out here! We want to hear him sing!" He'd go out there and start singing in the hallway.

My mother also sang around the house while she was doing things. She'd be singing with the radio, let's call it Doris Day and Eddie Fisher–type stuff. That's when I started singing. I sang the songs that were coming from the radio.

At P.S. 54, where I went to elementary school, I sang in school a couple of times when I was in fifth grade. They'd want me to come up in front [of] the class and sing. I remember it embarrassed me a little.

By the time I was seven or eight, I really didn't see any white people anywhere. It was all black and some were Spanish with dark skin. I didn't know if someone was Spanish unless I caught them speaking Spanish to someone. Other than that, they had no accent. These were just my friends, they were neighborhood people. Everybody spoke English. Nobody really spoke with any accents except Southern a little bit.

I started developing a street personality around the age of eleven or twelve. These were people I was around every day. I never thought about it or even consciously tried to emulate them. But when you're growing up in an area, it's natural that you're going to sound like your surroundings. By the time I was seven or eight, all I saw was black people. Some of them might have been Spanish. But I didn't see any white people.

Being white didn't stop us from being part of the neighborhood. As I got older and could move away from the stoop, I remember my mother opening the windows just like they show in old-fashioned movies and yelling. "Paul, Larry, get upstairs, it's seven o'clock! Get upstairs before I break your legs!" She doesn't know that you're involved in a street game. It could be ringolevio, or it could be a lot of things—slug, handball, things like that. You don't want to leave now you're in the midst of something.

"All right, I'll be right home!" you'd tell your mother. And she'd say, "You got ten minutes!" So my friends used to hear that, and they used to tease us. "Paul, you better get upstairs or your mother is going your break your legs!" But she wasn't that type of person; that was just the way she spoke. Everybody's parents had their little way of talking to their kids. It's time to eat, it's time to get upstairs, it's school tomorrow. All that stuff.

Like I said, I had a lot of fun growing up where I grew up. I didn't notice or ever wonder, where's the white people? I didn't think like that, and neither did my friends. They didn't address us as "you're white" or anything like that. We just took each other for granted. We just assumed, this is our block, our neighborhood.

At P.S. 54, where I started kindergarten when I was four, I saw white people here and there, and there were one or two black children in my class. I really stayed with black people because they were from my block. You went to school nearest where you lived, and you hung out with the people you saw after school. Half of the class was from my block. These were the people I dealt with, my own neighborhood people, from kindergarten all the way up [to] the sixth grade.

Around the age of twelve or thirteen, I started doing things to make money to buy my own stuff. One way was old fashioned, from even before I was born. You take a big jar with water and put a whisky glass inside the water jar. You take a shot, you drop a nickel in. If you get it in the glass, you get a dime back. If you don't, you lost your nickel, it's simple as that. You could also sell Kool-Aid; that's another thing I did. You'd go to the candy store and buy the little packets. You made a whole jug of it, threw sugar in it, and made it sweet. You stood in front [of] your building and put it on top of a milk crate. Let's say the glass was this big, that was five cents, ten cents, something like that. And that's how I accumulated a few dollars real early in life.

As I got older, my mind was inclined to things that were street hustles. I started hanging around people who did that. I don't mean bad people; it's just that they hustled in the streets.

I used to play numbers, and I made money with that. As I got older, I branched out a little more. Let's put it this way, I was the kind of kid who went out [of] the house with a couple decks of cards and craps. The nearest pool room was on Boston Road and Union Avenue. It was thirty-five cents an hour. And every neighborhood had a numbers man. We didn't call them bookies because that's what some of the white people were. When they made that hit, they came back through the block with big cars.

By the time I was thirteen or fourteen, I was a slick dresser. I kind of leaned toward the hustlers, the way they dressed. I was always around those kinds of people and used to go from pool room to pool room. I finally became a little better pool player. I wasn't a world beater, but I was a lot better than the average guy walking around the block. Those types of people dressed a certain way. They wore wingtips.

I got mine from Florsheim. The nearest Florsheim store was on Wilkins Avenue. When my father bought us shoes, he'd take us to the neighborhood army and navy store. We called them brogans. They were thick because he's thinking money. I hated them.

I spent my money on clothes, shoes, and to go to the movies. I always had to keep a certain amount of money in my pocket. Where you were known to be a hustler from the streets, no matter what your hustle was, you were a hustler. You had stickup guys, burglars, and gambling hustlers. I didn't think I had the guts to stick up anybody. But every neighborhood had its share of stickup kind of guys. Some of them got killed or went to jail, and some of them grew out of it. Back then they didn't kill you; they just took your money.

In my time on Jennings Street, a couple of people were murdered on the block. One time we heard that some cop threw somebody off the roof. I'll be honest with you. There was an occasional body found, but I don't remember too many times.

Further down from where we lived there were gangs. One time a guy from a gang came around looking for my brother. I don't know if he was crazy or he just had too much heart. He was in a gang called the Seven Crowns. Back then there was the Seven Crowns and the Bohemian Crowns. My brother was in the Bohemian Crowns, the only white kid in the gang.

I was in a gang called the Noble Kings and Queens because there were girls in the gang.

We were really a social club. We didn't go to gang fights. Once we were going to have a fight with a Spanish gang, but it never took place.

We didn't even get jackets. We gave dances, and house parties were a big thing. They used to call them the grind-'em-ups.

My girlfriends were mostly black, but there were white girls around. When I was growing up, it's a good thing I got to meet white people. A black girl from the neighborhood deliberately sent out word, "Find Paul and bring him to my house!" I said, "What for?" I was told, "She's having a party, and she wants to introduce you to somebody." I went to her house, and there was these two white girls. For some reason this black girl wanted to introduce me to white girls. It had nothing to do with racism. She just felt I needed to know white people.

There were always drugs around Jennings Street even before my time. Heroin was the big thing, even in the forties. I'd see guys nodding. They were the neighborhood guys. You knew who they were, and you didn't worry about them. That's what they did, but you ignored it. You knew them personally. You knew them when they were sober. It's not like you didn't know what they did, but it didn't affect your life.

They probably robbed apartments and did stuff like that, but they never robbed my house. They never robbed a lot of people's houses because they would have gotten their butt whipped. Sometimes they got killed trying to do something to get money, but I didn't see a massive number of people like that. There were a few alcoholics, but again, it wasn't in the multiples. So I never felt like this was a place that was unsafe, at least not for my family. It might have been to someone who wasn't from the neighborhood. But even those people we're talking about would come to your aid. They knew you their whole life.

I don't know why, but I always learned certain things fast. Scholastically inclined I was not, but in the street I was just better at some things. I picked up things fast as a kid. I wore my hat cocked to the side just like the older hustlers did. I could outtalk a lot of them. I call it sidewalk talk. I'd always have something to say. If you said something, I always had something to come back with.

I'd say thing like, "You back off or you fall off." Guys would say things like that. We just talked a lot of crap. What they call rap today was called crap then. You'd say something if someone was getting in your face or trying to be a wise guy.

I was a slow learner scholastically. It turned out that I'd been born with a disability. One teacher in elementary school took me under her wing and used to read to me at lunch hour. She was an ex–army sergeant. To keep us in line she used to tell us, "I was in the army, and I was a sergeant," and she wasn't going to take any stuff from us.

We didn't move from Morrisania; we were put out. My father fell on hard times. If it was a choice between food and the rent, he made sure we ate.

Back then the landlords wanted the rent on the first of the month. But paydays don't always fall on the first. Bottom line is this is how my family broke up. When I say broke up, I mean it was a bad time for my mother. Plus my brother Larry would steal if he had to in order to survive. Let's just say he could be a bodyguard kind of guy.

So we were evicted. All the furniture was put on the street, and my mother was crying, and the neighbors cried too. I really felt bad for her.

At seventeen I ended up living on my own. I always felt guilty that I hadn't become a famous singer because if I had, I might have gotten my family a house. Instead, I tried to make my money from the street. I could already play pool better than a lot of people. I could already cut games and get a percentage of it from the guy whose game it was, but I was just better because I used to entertain people with rhymes while I was dealing cards, like "Four treys, a miserable ways," "Five deuce, cut him loose," or in Cee-Lo, which was a game like blackjack, "He hid away, he'll have to play."

I was the kind of guy who was always rhyming. I rattled on and on. I even had to be protected a couple of times. The guy is losing his money, he doesn't want jokes about it. There was a barbershop where we used to have this game, and I'd say, "He threw four, he needs more," and go on and on. That's the way I cut games, always rhyming, so guys would say, if someone got upset, "My friends, it's a neighborhood thing." I could outdo a lot of guys when it came to that kind of stuff. It was natural for me, that's all. It still is. Even in the building on the Upper East Side where I work as a doorman, sometimes I just forget myself and start rhyming like I did back in the neighborhood.

Today I look at that kid Eminem, and all I think was that I used to do that for free. There wasn't a word I couldn't rhyme. I just did it automatically. I might be telling you something or giving some sort of advice. Whenever I told somebody something or explained something to someone, I did in a way that was entertaining. It just came naturally for me, that's all.

There were a lot of black people in my neighborhood—let's just use the term slicksters—and they could rap. But I went a little further. I'm not saying I was the best or anything. But I was good. I obviously got it from them, from growing up in that environment.

And from overhearing things. My singing, for instance, I used to sing things like "P.S. I Love You," and in the background I'd hear the radio. And when I started singing rock and roll in the beginning of the fifties, I started singing other peoples' songs because other groups were out already.

I kind of created my own style. I already had the accent of the neighborhood, whether I knew it or not. I didn't think of myself of having an accent. Somebody was always listening to me and saying, "Where are you from?" I'd say, "America. Where you think I'm from?" "Damn," they'd say. "You sound like you're from Georgia." Then I knew where they were coming from. And I'd say, "Well, I'm from the South, it's just called the South Bronx."

I never really took anything to heart. I was never insulted. I couldn't care less what people thought or if I didn't sound white enough for them. I didn't hate white people, don't get me wrong, I just didn't know any. And when I did get to know a couple of white people who heard about me through some black friends, it wasn't always easy for me, especially when the N word came into play.

That's not a word I was comfortable with. Even though the N word was used with affection by my neighborhood friends, I wouldn't reply in kind. I didn't like [it] because it was never meant to be a compliment.

I see white people doing it now with their black friends, and it's seems natural. I see teenagers, Spanish guys—and it's acceptable among friends because you're not really doing that cotton-picking stuff. These are your friends you hang out with, and the term would be used the way friends used it. I just never liked it because white people didn't make up that word to compliment you; it was to degrade you. It was as simple as that.

I'm talking about the South, of course, though as a kid I didn't know anything about that. I didn't know that black people sat at the back of the bus. When I was growing up in the Bronx, no one ever talked about that.

Race was never a problem when I was growing up—my race, their race, other races. It only became a problem when I started meeting white people. Because of the way they grew up, they'd use terms that I didn't like and didn't want to be associated with. Even with the guys I thought I could hang out with, if they said something that was negative, I'd say, "Hold up, Jack. Don't never say nothing like that because the people you're saying that to see us together, and to a person who doesn't know me who is not white, he sees me as being like that because I'm hanging with you."

If you're using the N word, or "spic," and using it negatively, I let them know how I feel. I say, "Stop the car, I'm getting out. You yelled out this, that, and the other, I'm in car with you, I look like you, and now that person believes I must think like you, and I can't allow that. I'll walk." My friend, an Italian dude, apologized to me. Then he tries to explain himself. He says because some black guys were bothering his girlfriend, he wanted to agitate them. "I don't care," I say. "This isn't about your girlfriend. I'm not here with you because somebody was bothering your girlfriend. Do not make it a race thing."

There were certain white guys who I felt I could hang out with. They would use those terms in their conversation, and I'd say, "You can't do that with me, Jack," and I'd walk away. "Oh, man, I'm sorry," they'd say. "I didn't mean nothing like that. I was just telling a story." Then I'd say, "I told you, man, my family is that way. You want to see the UN, meet my nieces and nephews. That's how we married."

I was with a black girl, and my next one was black, and my next one. Actually, the woman I married was a white girl who I met after I got to know certain white dudes that I could hang around with. And some of them also were hustlers, in the same way that I hustled. There were some people I felt were cool.

I always used a term for white guys. "They were all right for white guys." It didn't mean they didn't use certain words, but they'd respect me, and if they did it in front of me, they'd say, "Oh, man, I'm sorry, I forgot you were here. I know you don't like that."

Once I got to know white people, I was around them a lot. Like I said, all I knew when I was growing up was black and Spanish people, and if that's all you see every day of your life in school, out of school, on the block, you don't even know it, but you're getting an accent. The only time you really know you got an accent is when someone unlike you hears you. They're looking at you, they're wondering, where are you from? Because they see a white guy, but when they close their eyes they hear a black guy.

I've been threatened by cops because of the company I kept when I was growing up. I've had a cop yell out the car, "I'm going to get you!" and I looked over at my friend who was black, and I'd say, "I wonder what the hell did I do? Why is he telling me that?" I didn't realize till later on it's because of where I am. He saw me as a white guy who probably didn't live in the neighborhood. It never dawned on the cop that maybe I was born here and grew up here and lives down the block. He's thinking, "Why is he here? He must be here to get drugs."

I had a rough life; I was poor as a young adult. I was homeless before it was in style. They didn't have shelters because I could have damn sure have used one. I remember walking in a blizzard just to get five dollars from a friend. I walked past Pelham Parkway all the way to University Avenue for five dollars. I didn't blame nobody; that's just the way life was.

There were black families that had more than us. I used to go to this guy's house just to play with his toys. He had good toys and stuff like that because he was an only child.

I didn't dislike white people. They just weren't there. I wasn't prejudiced against whites. My family isn't prejudiced against anybody for what they are because we don't have those hangups in my family. When I say my family is the UN, I mean it. I've got nieces and nephews who are Cuban, Dominican, Puerto Rican, African. These are my nieces and nephews, and they outnumber us. The only ones we didn't hook up with were the Irish.

I married a girl who recently died, but who was part Irish, part Spaniard. But if you were to ask her family, well, what are you, they'd always 'fess up to the fact that Irish was the one they favored. I remember when we were going to get married, the candy store lady in her neighborhood on Tremont Avenue, she said, "My daughter is getting married to this Jewish guy. Can't you do something about that?"

Let me put it this way, we'd probably all be considered poor white trash. You can take them out [of] the neighborhood, but you can't take the neighborhood out of them. I guess in some ways I'm like that. I'm out of the neighborhood as far as living there goes, but I go back to see my friends, who are grandparents now, and we all meet there.

Some of them still play numbers. I do too occasionally. And we stand around, in summer especially, and just rap about the old days, and sometimes we'll look at some of the young people doing something that didn't look too good. "Look at that," we say. "We didn't do that. Look what he's doing."

I'd say, "See, remember when our parents used to say things like that? Look what we're saying, and we're our parents' age now." We used to say, "Oh, I'll never talk like that!" That's why I keep an open mind even when it comes to today's music, rap and stuff like that.

There are young people I speak to sometimes. They're always asking me questions about the era I grew up in and wondering why I talk the way I do. When push comes to shove, I'm more comfortable around the block. Even on my job sometimes, when I'm comfortable with people, my street personality comes out. When one of the tenants in the building calls me on the intercom, I sometimes say, "Your call, I'm Paul, what do you want?" Or, "It's your dime and my time."

I'm not being disrespectful. I know who's calling me, and I know they'll get a kick out of it because they don't expect to hear someone saying the things I say. One tenant said, "I could have sworn I was talking to a black guy." I said, "Well, in some ways you are."

Toys? Let me tell you something. I remember standing on line at the police precinct for a checkerboard game. You know, at Christmas time. I got called out at my class, "Himmelstein, go down to the third floor and see Mrs. So and So." They'd never say what it's for. It might be the dean or something, and I'd be thinking, what the hell do they want?

And there was always a room, even today I'm sure they have it, under the stairwell or something. Where donations came in, like clothing, and we were the kind of family that we got free shoes. It was a 600 school, a school where they transferred you from the neighborhood school when they considered you a bad kid.

At a certain time of the year they would notify certain families, "Here, take this home to your mother," and "Bring this back, she has to sign this." What it turned out to be is, you're going to go to 612, and you get free shoes. We used to get, like, brand-new shoes, it wasn't a hand-me-down thing. I never forgot things like that, brand-new shoes. Not stylish, just brand new.

And I remember in P.S. 54 being called out the class at times and told, "Himmelstein, go to the second floor, see so-and-so teacher." And they'd take me into this room, and there'd be all kinds of clothing lying around. Used clothes, and try this on, try this coat on, try that on.

Sometimes there was some nice stuff because it came from people who were well off, and it was stylish. I also grew up getting things from people in our family. We had parts of the family, uncles and stuff who were doing better, and they only had two kids. And when they bought next year's new stuff for their kids or the kids grew out of things, they'd call our house and say, "Send the boys over; we got a box of clothes."

I remember going to my aunts' and uncles' house, and they'd have a couple of boxes, and we'd bring them back to my house and look

through them. And whoever something fit, it fit. Occasionally something would fit two of us—it might be a nice jacket or something—and
here comes the fight.

You grew up that way; you don't think of yourself as poor. I never
thought of myself as poor, but obviously we were poor, except we
weren't hungry poor.

Let's just say my college was the street. In school I didn't have a shot.
I wasn't scholastically inclined. I had to read dirty books to learn to read.

In school I always tried to get out of things because everybody could
read. School for me was humiliating. I'm not knocking school, mind
you, but you have to look at it from the kid's point of view. When you
can't do something everybody else can do, scholastically speaking, it's
constantly humiliating. And you have to do this every single day.

So when you're in school you have to be very cunning to keep it a
secret that you can't read. And sometimes you can't get out of it. For
years, every time it was my time to read out loud, I would yell, "I gotta
go to the bathroom!" And when you see it's going to be your row that
was going to be asked to read, you said, "Oh, shit!" We all had the book,
and you each read a paragraph. Some kids could read better than other
kids, but I was the kid that could barely read at all. I read very slowly. I
had to study each word.

But you can't read aloud like that. You got to read it, and then you're
trying to pronounce it correctly. Sometimes you made a mistake, sometimes you got lucky, but most of the time you were wrong. Nobody
bothered to find out if I or anyone else in my family had a problem
and try to correct it, like they do today. So if you had a problem, you
tried to hide it because even among your friends, everybody took it for
granted everyone can read and write. I had a brother who couldn't read,
I mean at all. And he was married with kids.

Everything I picked up, I did it on my own. School didn't teach me. I
taught me. Now I'm no genius at reading. I can read a newspaper and
things like that. I spell better, but again, I'm not college material. So I
really didn't give a damn that I was asked to leave school. I consider that
a break because I was in high school then, and I didn't even learn what
I should have learned in junior high. But that's how it went when you
grew up in the forties and fifties. If you had a problem, you fell through
the cracks.

I was always forced to be cunning, to protect my pride and prevent
myself from being looked at as stupid. I never felt stupid. Yet in those

days, to your peers who could pick up a book and read and all that, you're stupid if you can't. But you could be smarter than them. There's different kinds of smart. You could be a genius kind of person just because you have common sense. I know people that I've given common-sense advice on certain issues. They may have been way ahead of me scholastically, but they couldn't handle certain things. They could read books, but I had to be very cunning and have common sense to survive.

From the time when I was seventeen and became homeless, I was on my own. The first thing I did was go to the pool hall and start hustling and make real money so I could live in a furnished room. Back then, real money was like $10 depending on the size of the room. You could get a real good room for $20 a week. And you could make that kind of money in the neighborhood.

There were rooming houses. If you got a room and you're paying $20 or $25, you got a kitchenette. Thank God I can laugh at it now, but I've lived in places with just enough room for a bed, a dresser, and that was home to me. I lived that way from the time I was seventeen into my twenties, and there were times when I didn't make enough to make room rent. You had your bad days too.

Even if you're good at something, sometimes you just couldn't make any money that particular week, and it's rent time every week when you got a furnished room. You'd have to go. I'd take whatever little possessions I had and put them somewhere where they could be kept safe, in somebody's house or something, until I made enough money in the streets to get another room. And until then I slept on roofs, rooftops. And I never blamed anybody because my life is nobody's fault. It's the way life went.

I like to think that I turned out okay. I walked down streets until I could make money my way. I wasn't going to hit nobody in no head for money. There's a lot of ways to be smart. I don't consider myself no genius, but it's like a blind person who hears better than you and me because they can't see.

It works the same for people who are not scholastically inclined. They can be smarter than you. You can be gifted with the mouth. You can fix anything. You're not a carpenter, you're not a plumber, but you know a little bit about everything. With your hands you're good, and you can make money that way. And that's that.

Joseph Orange

Joseph Orange (1941–), a professional trombone player for many years, recently retired as a vice president of Blue Cross/Blue Shield.

My family moved to Prospect Avenue and 168th Street in Morrisania in 1941, the year I was born. They'd moved there from Harlem, where they lived right behind the Apollo Theater on 126th Street. I'm the youngest in my family of nine, and my older brothers and sisters, who were already in their teens when we moved to the Bronx, spent a lot of time reminiscing about growing up on 126th Street.

We had only three bedrooms, but fortunately, because of the spread of age, we were never all there at the same time. When I was four, my brother was off in the army. I never remember all of us living there together, but I do remember us sharing rooms. My two sisters had a room together. My two brothers. I was the baby, so I was always out on the couch somewhere.

My father worked for the Union News Company, which owned newspaper stands and restaurants in Manhattan, and he was a Gullah. The Gullah culture is from South Carolina, from one of the Sea Islands, and unfortunately my father died when I was only four so I don't have a very vivid memory of him. But my older brothers and sisters said he spoke the Gullah language and that his English was difficult to understand because of that mixture of West Indian, African, and Southern.

My mother, who was seventeen when she married my father, was from a small town outside Atlanta called Social Circle, Georgia. I didn't visit that town until about five years ago, when we had a family reunion and we went back to Social Circle to see where my mother was born and the church where she was baptized.

My parents met in the South when my father was working in Atlanta, and they lived in Savannah, Georgia, for a while before moving to New York. They were married for about fifteen years before they had any children, but then they had children one after another.

There were a number of musicians on my mother's side of the family. My mother had a brother named J. C. Higginbotham, and in the thirties and forties he was considered the top jazz trombone player in the world. If you listen to the original version of Louis Armstrong playing "When the Saints Go Marching In," the first time that song was ever recorded in the thirties, on that recording you'll hear him saying, "Here comes brother Higginbotham walking down the aisle."

My uncle plays the famous jazz trombone solo on that recording. He went on to play with Armstrong, and he played with Fletcher Henderson, who led one of the premier jazz bands of the 1930s. Later in his career he spent many years with Henry Red Allen, another Bronxite. Henry Red Allen lived a block from me, and they played for years at the Metropole Café at Forty-Eighth and Broadway in Manhattan. As a kid, I can remember when my uncle was staying at our house, and Allen would drive by in his Cadillac and honk his horn and pick up my uncle so he could go to work. Sometimes he'd come up and have a drink with my uncle, and they'd sit and chat.

J. C.'s niece, my mother's first cousin, was a woman by the name of Irene Higginbotham. She was a songwriter and arranger and piano player, and back in the 1940s she wrote a lot of songs for Billie Holliday and other top jazz singers of that time. Her notable song was "Good Morning Heartache."

Irene actually lived in my house for years, and J. C. was always coming and going. Whenever he came to New York he stayed at my house, sometimes for months at a time. He was very close to my mother. So I'd see J. C. at least once a week, and Irene actually lived with us when I was a kid. Later she got married and moved to Brooklyn, but she always remained very close to my mother.

One of my earliest recollections is 1945, the year World War II ended. I was just a kid, but I remember that everybody was out on the street, yelling, "We won the war! The war is over!" There was a big celebration, a lot of people out, and I paraded around shouting, "We won the war! We won the war!" I remember wandering down the street to the end of the block and not having my mother in sight and being scared because I was on my own for the first time. I guess I was four years old, but as a kid, particularly in the 1940s, the Bronx seemed like the biggest and safest place in the world. I had this sense of security because everyone knew me. I hope this isn't a false memory because it seems real to me.

I could never get in any trouble even if I wanted to because some neighbor would be bringing me back to my mother, saying, "I saw your son doing so and so." We lived in a five-story tenement with four apartments on each floor, and to this day I could tell you the names of every person in every apartment in that building. Five times four is twenty families, and you figure four or five people in each family because there were some large families, including my own. But I could name every person who lived there.

The building was mostly African American, but later I recall a few Puerto Rican families. There were a couple of two-parent families, but mostly it was single females raising their children.

I went to P.S. 99, which was a block and a half away. I can only recall two African American teachers, and I didn't have either one of them. But the teachers who were there were so dedicated, so committed, so nurturing. Back in those days we had a tracking system. If you were in 5–1, for example, you were very smart, and if you were in 5–15 you were not so smart. I was fortunate because I was always in the 1 classes. Maybe we got all this attention and nurturing and excellent training because we were the smartest kids. I don't know.

My siblings were always in the 1 classes too. When I started school, and this was a real disadvantage in some ways, all the teachers knew me because my brothers and sisters had preceded me. If you were in the Orange family, you were expected to be a good student.

When I was in the eighth grade, I started to move with the wrong crowd. I started to run around with some kids who were definitely not headed in any positive direction, and we'd go to the P.S. 99 community center. I never did all the things they were doing, but I was there. And I'll never forget one day I [was] walking out of the center, and the director of the center, a wonderful mentor by the name of Vincent Tibbs, grabbed me by the arm, put his arm around me, and said, "Joe, it's time for you to cut these guys loose." I said, "What do you mean? These are my buddies." And he said, "No, I know the Orange family too well. You're going in a different direction."

That's all he ever said to me, and at the time it didn't impress me. But later I thought about it, and I mention that experience as an example of how there were adults in the community who knew you, who knew your family, and who observed you.

Another reason my family had this high standard that so many people in the neighborhood recognized had to do with my mother. Even though she had eight children and our father died when I was very young, she had come from a prominent family in Georgia where everyone was educated and musically talented. Music was a big part of our household. As a family every Christmas we'd sing Christmas carols. Neighbors would come in. My sisters were dancers and singers, and my brother was a singer.

Within the family the number-one expectation was that you'd be a good musician. And my mother had this real sense of pride about her children. We had a certain respect in the neighborhood because even the bad guys, if they saw me doing something bad, would say, "No, Joe, not you."

I started playing an instrument in seventh grade, when I was eleven. I'd been surrounded by music. I could sing. Even in P.S. 99 I remember standing on stage and singing. We didn't have a chorus or anything like that, but I do recall an auditorium. Certain kids would get up and perform, and I was one of those kids.

Growing up, I also played every conceivable type of ball—softball, baseball, stoop ball, punch ball, dodge ball, or dodge the ball. When I was very young, six or seven, I used to run behind my older brothers. They'd play baseball and softball in the backyard, and they organized these leagues. They'd actually have all-star games, and only the best players would get into the all-star games and "World Series," when you'd have one team playing against another in a series of best of seven, that type of thing.

Even before I could participate in these games on my own, my older brothers were always babysitting me. So I was along for the ride, hanging out in the backyard. And I remember that around the corner from our street was 168th Street, which was paved with cobblestones. Imagine trying to play softball and baseball on cobblestone streets, but we did.

Saturday was movie day. I think movies cost a dime. The three movie theaters I remember in the area were the Prospect Theater, which was a little further down on Prospect Avenue, near the Prospect Avenue train station. There was Loew's, which we used to call LOW-ees, which was near Fordham Road, and there was an RKO theater on Prospect Avenue. There was also a fourth theater up on Boston Road near 168th called the Tower Theater. To this day, I don't know exactly what went on at the movie theater, but it had a bad reputation, and my mother wouldn't let me go there.

When I was growing up, there were certain areas you were told to avoid, blocks that were particularly tough, like Home Street, around the corner from where I lived. Home Street was an area where I didn't venture. I knew a lot of people from that area, and they were tough. Even at a very young age they were tough. Not everyone, of course: Herbert Coleman, who was a child star and a singer, lived on Home Street. He's one of my closest friends today. Tim Henderson, who got a Ph.D. in physics, grew up on Home Street too.

My first formal music school introduction came when I went to J.H.S. 40. When we were in the sixth grade—I think it was only those kids in 1 and 2 classes—we were given a music aptitude test. If we passed the test and our academic grades were acceptable, we were put into what they called special music classes at J.H.S. 40 in seventh grade. They also had special art classes for kids who were talented in art.

The test was basically, can you recognize a pitch, what notes are higher than this one, lower than this one, pretty basic stuff. Then when you arrived at J.H.S. 40, you were allowed to select your own instrument and begin your musical training. And you could take your instrument home. I picked the trombone because my uncle was a famous trombone player, and I thought if I studied the instrument he might give me my own trombone.

You had an hour of English, an hour of math, an hour of music, and so on. There was also a dance band, an orchestra, a concert band, a chorus, and a drama club. In the eighth grade they decided to mix the music class and the drama class. They got rid of the drama club and decided that one class would do both music and drama. Eighth grade was my favorite year of all my education because all we did was put on plays and play music. We did *Carmen Jones*; we did *Of Thee I Sing*. I remember big productions, and the art department would do the backdrops. I had great times, but we were kept out of class a lot, and so we missed a lot of fundamentals of algebra and other academics.

The teachers realized that this program was more than just enrichment and that there might be truly talented people coming out of this program. We had one kid who lived on Prospect Avenue. Her name was Carol Jefferson; she was playing concerts in kindergarten. She was a child prodigy. By the time she got to J.H.S. 40, she was already well known. Her mother had to take her out of school a lot to play concerts. She went to the High School of Performing Arts and finally got a degree from Juilliard. Today, she has a Ph.D. in music, and she plays concerts all over Europe. But she was playing at the age of four, so they knew that there was some talent there.

I also had my little interlude of rebellion. I wasn't in a gang when I was growing up, but there were gangs, and some of them seemed quite dangerous. I don't remember if there were any real murders, but I wouldn't be surprised if there were.

I remember one big fight. I was in the eighth or ninth grade. It's 1953 or 1954, and on the Fourth of July I went off with my bad friends to Pelham Bay Park for the day. I didn't know it at the time, but Pelham Bay Park had been taken over by two gangs, the Sportsmen and the Seven Crowns. They were supposed to be meeting at the park to have this big rumble to determine who was the premier gang of the Bronx.

I was wearing a red shirt, and the uniform for the Sportsmen was black pants and a red shirt. I was afraid one of these Seven Crowns would see me and think I was a Sportsman. I was really scared and wanted to get out of there, but I didn't know how to tell my friends that I wanted to go home.

To be a bad kid in my neighborhood meant that we left the neighborhood and we'd ride our bicycles up to the Bronx Zoo or Bronx Park and go swimming in the polluted lake. It was at Bronx Park that what was probably the worst incident occurred. We rode our bicycles up to the park, left the area where the little lake was, went along some wooded dirt paths, and we ran into a couple of white boys. I was kind of trailing behind, and by the time I got up to the pack, they were assaulting these two boys. I remember this one boy, Leon Gray, saying remember Emmett Till, the black kid who had been murdered in Mississippi when he was fourteen, because that Emmett Till thing had just happened.

I don't think anyone thought much of it. It was just something to do. Afterwards we got back on our bicycles and started riding, and we ended up on the other side of the park, which was an all-white area. And all of the sudden we were surrounded by police cars.

We were all arrested, and they took us to a police station. We had to sit and wait and wait until our parents came. So finally my mother comes, and my uncle had happened to be by the house that day, and he came in and introduced himself to one of the policemen and said, "I'm J. C. Higginbotham." The policeman was a jazz fan, and he said, "J. C. Higginbotham, what are you doing here?" And my uncle said, "My nephew is here." And somehow I escaped going to court with the other boys. I just happened to have a family that carried a little weight.

But I don't recall a lot of racial tension in the Bronx at that time. My classes were about fifty-fifty black and white, and I don't ever remember a racial incident. A lot of my friends weren't African American. My best friend through junior high school was a kid by the name of Fred Sadona, and he was Italian. Fred Sadona was the commissioner of the school, the top position that any student could hold. He ran against an African American kid, the student body voted, and he won. But after sixth or seventh grade, I don't remember seeing any of the white kids after school, even though we were in school together. Even Fred Sadona. I don't remember him coming to my house or me going to his house.

I remember two eras of talent shows at P.S. 99. When I was younger I'd go with my older sisters and brothers. My older brother always performed because he was a singer. He was a pop singer, like Billy Eckstine, and later he actually joined a group. They made a couple of records, and he was the lead singer, but nothing much came of it.

In the pre-doo-wop era, the people who performed at the talent shows were my older brothers and sisters and individual performers. The emcee was a guy named Leroy Gordon, who sounded just like Satchmo. I remember a tap dancer named Gene Paige and a guy who played the bongos. That was in the early fifties. Then in my era came the doo-wop groups. It would just be one doo-wop group after another. I was never part of a group. I just sang in the hallways with my buddies.

The Orange reputation preceded me into high school. I had a brother, Freddie, who was a singer. After J.H.S. 40 he went to Music and Art and was just beginning his professional career as a singer and dancer.

I had another brother, David, who was six years older than me who played and who was an athlete, a wonderful athlete. He played every sport, but he really excelled at boxing. He was a Golden Gloves Champion and got to the finals in the Olympic trials, but he lost that one fight, so he didn't go to the Olympics.

In my opinion, the teachers at Morris High School recognized those of us who were talented or serious about wanting to do something, and they'd extend themselves to no end to support us. It was at Morris that I was really encouraged to take my music seriously and start studying. I had a couple of music teachers there who would let me cut my other classes to play music. It was just amazing.

A lot of my friends went to Music and Art. They got a good education, but they were not encouraged to play jazz. It was all classical. That was not the case at Morris. If you wanted to play jazz, it was fine. Once I tried to do some arranging, and I showed what I did to one of my teachers, and one day he used his lunch break to show me how to score things.

We had one teacher who was actually writing hit songs in the doo-wop vein. He used to go down to Fifty-Second Street every day after school to peddle his songs. Every day he'd say, "Joe, what do you think of this?" And every day he'd have a new rock and roll song.

I began getting instruction outside of school in the eleventh grade. I had a friend who went to Morris who wanted to be a trumpet player. He wasn't that talented as a trumpet player, but he knew a lot of people, and he said, "Joe, if you're serious about being a musician, you have to practice." He introduced me to a trombone player who was about six years older than me, and he agreed to teach me. I'd go by his house two or three days a week, and we'd play duets, and he'd show me different things. This was free, no charge.

I practiced at home four, five, six hours a day. This was in a tenement, with the windows open, but I never remember complaints. Maybe this [was] because there was noise and music everywhere. There was a record store on the corner that played their music outside. I never remember it as being an issue.

I first became aware of Latin music in high school because a lot of my friends had started venturing out to Latin venues and go dancing, and they'd come to school and say we heard Tito Puente and we heard Tito Rodriguez. They'd be talking about all this Latin music, and I started to pay attention to it. The big thing was the Palladium, at Fifty-Third Street and Broadway. There were also a lot of places in the neighborhood. I didn't go to them, but the Puerto Ricans had a lot of dance clubs.

There was also West Indian music. I had a friend, Richie Powell, who played drums, and he always had a band. He wasn't the best musician, but he was the most entrepreneurial. He was the guy who'd get the jobs. I remember going by his house, and he had steel drums. That was the first time I'd ever seen them. My sister married a West Indian so I was aware of the Mighty Sparrow and West Indian music, but I didn't consider this to be the hip music. I wouldn't buy a West Indian album.

In high school, I became very serious about my music. I was playing my music outside of the community. I was playing in groups downtown. I was playing with a lot of kids who went to Music and Art and the High School of the Performing Arts. I got connected with them through neighborhood people like Jimmy Owens, who went to Music and Art.

I knew Jimmy from kindergarten. He was one of those rare individuals who the first time he picked up his instrument he knew he wanted to be a musician. I wasn't like that at all. Anyway, Jimmy and I started venturing out of the neighborhood, playing a lot of music all over the city, anywhere we could play, and I became focused exclusively on music.

In high school I didn't have a wide social circle. I didn't have a group of people I ran with. I just had the one or two people who were serious about music. In some respects I missed a lot of the traditional high school experience. My senior year of high school I played at the Newport Jazz Festival, and I missed my graduation because I had to go to rehearsal.

The group I played with was called the Newport Youth Band. A notice had gone out to every high school in the city that George Wein had hired a band director named Marshall Brown to form a band that would appear at the Newport Jazz Festival every year and play around the United States. I went to audition, and there were eight hundred students trying out for the eighteen positions. I didn't try out, but a year later there was an opening, and through Jimmy Owens, who was already in the band, they called me and I went to play and got accepted.

There were other Bronx kids in the band, and they all became professional musicians. One was Al Abreu, who lived across the street from St. Augustine's Church. He went on to play with Mongo Santamaria, Tito Puente, and Hugh Masekela. That's Al Abreu playing saxophone on "Grazing in the Grass."

Then there was Harry Hall, who lived on 167th Street and had gone to P.S. 99 and J.H.S. 40. He became a jazz trumpet soloist, and we played together in Lionel Hampton's band and in Lloyd Price's band. There was a white kid who lived on Allerton Avenue, near the Bronx Zoo, named Larry Morton. He was a saxophone player who had a career as a professional musician. Then there was me and Jimmy. So out of eighteen kids there were five of us from a relatively small area in the Bronx.

When I was in the Newport Youth Band, I was living in the Bronx. But we could only stay in the band until our nineteenth birthday, so afterward I moved downtown with a friend of mine, a bass player. We got an apartment on Seventy-Eighth Street near Amsterdam Avenue, and I started my musical career. I spent two years being a struggling jazz artist. The bass player I lived with was friends with another trombone player named Barry Rogers, who was also from the Bronx and who went on to become one of the greatest Latin trombone players in the history of Latin music even though he wasn't Latin.

My friend said to me, "Joe, I want you to hear this guy Barry Rogers play." So we went up to the Triton Club in the Bronx, a Latin music club near Hunts Point Palace. It was actually an after-hours place, but they would get major people. I remember seeing Celia Cruz, Arsenio Rodriguez, some major Latin artists.

So I went up to hear this guy Barry Rogers and Eddie Palmieri play, and I met Barry. He said they had two trombones, and the other trombone player, Mark Weinstein, was going to Europe. "If you want to come and try out for the band," he said, "I'll give you a call when Mark leaves in a couple of months."

A month later I got a call from Barry Rogers, and he says, "Joe, do you want to come and try out for the band we're playing at?" They were playing at a place in Harlem on 125th Street. It was Eddie Palmieri's band, so I tried out, got the job, and ended up playing with Barry and Eddie Palmieri for the next year and a half.

We played Wednesday, Thursday, Friday, Saturday. Usually on Friday, Saturday, and Sunday nights, we played two jobs, sometimes two night jobs. On Sunday we played a matinee. A typical Friday night, we'd play a set in the Bronx, pack up, jump in our cars, drive out to Brooklyn, and play at another place in Brooklyn. Or we'd play the Palladium and then pack up and come up to the Bronx and play the Broadway Casino.

After I left Eddie Palmieri, I decided to do a rhythm and blues and soul thing. I wanted to travel, and a friend of mine who was playing trombone with Lloyd Price asked me if I wanted to play with him. At the time I thought of traveling as glamorous and fun. I learned very quickly that I'd made a huge mistake, but I did join Lloyd Price. This was after most of his big hits. The only hit he recorded while I was there was "Misty."

He was playing the chitlin circuit. We played the Apollo, we played the Howard Theater in Washington, D.C., the one in Philadelphia, and a lot of venues throughout the South. I'd never been further south than New Jersey.

It was a very talented group. The leader of the band was Slide Hampton, and prior to him you had Al Gray. Slide Hampton and Al Gray were monster trombone players, much more advanced than me, and I learned a tremendous amount playing with them.

After that I went to Lionel Hampton's band. At the time I was living with my mother on Prospect Avenue. This was the mid-sixties, and a lot of people I grew up with were beginning to use drugs. The guys in my eighth-grade group, all of those guys started to fool around with heroin. When I'd come off the road, I'd ask about somebody, and people would say, "Oh, he's strung out. He's strung out."

Ten years earlier you could leave your door open in the summer to get cross-ventilation between the back door and the front window. That was no longer possible. I'd come home at night, get off at Prospect [Avenue] station, and walk the six or seven blocks to the apartment. I had my trombone, and I had to keep my eyes open because it was two or three in the morning.

After working with Lionel Hampton, I went to Herbie Mann's band, and I stayed with Herbie until 1966. We traveled all over the world. We went to Japan, Europe, South America. That was the best gig I ever had because Herbie treated his musicians well, and we traveled well. I got on that band, and then I got Jimmy hired on that band.

After two years with Herbie, I decided to move to California and go to school. This is 1966, 1967. I stayed there for a year and a half and came back and stayed with my mother until I could find a place to live in New York. That's when I really noticed the change in the neighborhood, maybe because I'd been away for so long. I'd see kids I knew from elementary school nodding on the street corners, people robbing each other, people who were friends robbing each other for drugs. People like my mother and my friends' parents were afraid to leave their houses. I'd ask about people, and they'd say this one had died from an overdose, this one was in jail. It was like a horrible plague had killed the neighborhood.

There were so many individual tragedies. One of my very close friends, a kid named Gordon Vinyl, one of the most brilliant people I ever met—this kid was reading Plato in elementary school—but he got involved in drugs, and all his sisters and brothers were involved in drugs.

I remember looking out the window at my mother's house onto Prospect Avenue. Gordon walked by, and I go down, and we started chatting, and he says, "Why don't you come up to my mother's house? That's where we all hang out, all the old guys." His family had moved to Crotona Avenue, and that's when I saw a lot of my old friends from elementary school. And they were all using heroin. It was the most depressing thing. Drugs weren't completely foreign to me being a musician, but this was very sad. Almost without exception all of those people are dead now.

I don't remember that my mother worried about people in the building robbing her. She was very respected. Even the drug addicts respected my mom a little bit. I never felt that any of those kids I knew would harm my mother, desperate as they were.

After staying with my mother for a little, I found an apartment in the Soundview area. I was playing, doing weekends with different Latin bands, I wasn't practicing much. I was really thinking about getting out of the business. Then I met a woman, fell in love, got married, and moved to Staten Island.

That's where I was living when the building I grew up in burned in the early seventies. I got a call from a guy named Freddy Pettus. He and Jimmy Owens and I were best friends. Freddie lived on 168th Street, right around the corner from my mother's building. He called me one evening and told me that my mother's building was on fire. She had abandoned the house, and he had brought a chair for her to sit in and a blanket to keep her warm.

So I went over to the building. It wasn't demolished, but it was damaged beyond repair. Our apartment was mostly smoke damaged. There hadn't been a lot of direct fire, but it certainly wasn't livable. We made arrangements for my mother to stay with one of my sisters. I came back the next day with one of my brothers to see what we could salvage. People had come in and started to take things out of the house, so my brother decided he would stay there.

I don't know how he managed to do this because it was really horrible, no lights, nothing. But he stayed just to keep people out while we could make other arrangements and get the stuff out. We managed to salvage some things, but certain things [that] should have been there were missing. I lost my favorite electric train set.

I believe that the fire was arson. My mother had been warned. During the day someone had knocked on her door and said, "Ms. Orange, I think there's going to be a fire here today. I smell smoke. Something is going on in this building. I don't know if it's electrical." I think he wanted her to get out.

I never came back to the old neighborhood after my mother left. I stayed away from the Bronx because the Bronx to me was very depressing. By then it was the seventies, and I'd moved up to Elmsford in Westchester.

I could have gone back. I had plenty of opportunities. When I was living in Elmsford I was working in Manhattan, so I took the commuter train. But it's very painful to go back to the place where you spent so many years of your life, where you have so many pleasant memories, and you don't see anyone you know, and people are looking at you as if you're an outsider. Everything familiar and positive about the area is gone. P.S. 99 is not open. We had a vegetable store, a grocery store, two pharmacies, a candy store, a barber shop. All of this stuff within a block of where you lived, and all of it is just gone. All the stores are sitting empty.

In the seventies, which was the one time I drove through the neighborhood, there were still a few buildings that were occupied and a couple of people sitting on the stoop. I tried to see if there was anyone I recognized, but everyone I knew had long gone. So it wasn't a pleasant experience. I don't know if it would be a pleasant experience today.

I know they have a Bronx reunion every year. Thousands of people come to Crotona Park. My brother goes, and every year he calls me and says, "Joe I saw this one and I saw that one," and he tells me all the people he saw, and I'm still wrestling with whether I want to go.

I think that being born and raised in the Bronx, whatever I am, whoever I am, being a Bronxite is part of it. I even have a baseball cap that I wear when I travel around. Whenever we go on cruises or travel around the world, I wear this hat that says, "Bronx." And it's amazing the people I meet. Hundreds of people, no exaggeration. "Bronx!" they say.

I think the Bronx is a unique place, like some other historical places you've read about where African Americans achieved a great deal that has been written out of history. I think the Bronx is in danger of being like that.

There was a great deal of achievement. People had personal successes, and that doesn't happen in a vacuum. That happens because of family, it happens because of community, it happens because of school, it happens because of churches. It happens for a multitude of reasons, and all those reasons existed in that community at that time. It's troubling to me that it all disappeared, and there's some guilt too.

There were a lot of famous people in the neighborhood. I used to see Thelonious Monk walk down Prospect Avenue, and he wasn't the only one. I have a funny story about this. When Jimmy Owens and I were kids, we used to play marbles and yo-yos on 168th Street. On several occasions, this guy would come by, and he'd visit somebody who lived in the tall building on the side of the street that was all brownstones.

In that building lived a family called the Clark family. I was friends with the son and daughter, Carol Clark and Gwendolyn Clark. And this guy would always come and visit the family. Later, when we're in high school, and we're starting to read and explore music, we got on this Langston Hughes kick. We started reading all of his books. And we heard that Langston Hughes was giving a poetry reading and a book signing at St. Augustine's Church.

So I told Jimmy and my friend Freddy, and the three of us went down to St. Augustine's and were very surprised to see that Langston Hughes was the guy we'd been seeing since we were kids, visiting this family on 168th Street. He'd always stop and play with the kids. He was very good with the yo-yo, and he'd show us tricks. We never knew it was Langston Hughes, but Mr. Clark, who lived on 168th Street and Prospect Avenue, was his brother.

On the corner of Union Avenue and 168th Street there was Tyree Glenn, the famous trombone player, and he had a television show at that time. And of course, Erroll Garner lived on Intervale Avenue. He lived in a tenement directly across the street from my friend Ron Nelson. I've been told that W. C. Handy lived on Union Avenue in the Bronx, but I don't know that for a fact. And some of these people actually participated in the community. I remember that a famous jazz saxo-phone player named Lou Donaldson came by on at least one occasion and played with us at P.S. 99 Community Center. He played with Miles Davis.

Not everybody became a musician or an athlete. My friend Tim Henderson was the neighborhood brain growing [up]. We used to tease Tim unmercifully because he was so smart and he wore glasses.

He wanted to be an athlete. He played on all of the teams. But he made it into the Bronx High School of Science, which was rare at that time, and went on to earn his Ph.D. in physics and became a physicist and inventor. He's retired now, and lives near Ann Arbor, Michigan, and he's got a lab in his house.

One thing that helped people like us was that there were older guys and people in the neighborhood who cared enough to give something back. In my case I was fortunate to have an older brother who was always keeping me up nights, talking to me and telling me which guys to watch out for.

I can remember summer nights, the two of us just sitting and chatting, and he'd say, "You have to pick your role models very carefully because there are a lot of guys around here who are not very good role models, and most of your friends seem to be picking them because those are the guys that are running numbers and selling drugs. And yes, they have the cars, and yes, they have the fancy clothes."

If I lived on Prospect Avenue today, I don't know if anyone could point out ten people and say, "This one is going to school. This one is a doctor. This one is a lawyer." And that's unfortunate. One of the questions about some of the Bronx communities today is where do they find those role models? Who's there to give them free trombone lessons? Who's there to start a baseball team? Who's running a community center or giving them instruments to take home from school? It's like society has abandoned them.

It shouldn't be that kids growing up in the forties and fifties had more than kids growing up in the Bronx today. I agonize a little over it.

I don't want to idolize the way it was when I was growing up. It wasn't all pretty. Even on the best days there was some bad stuff going on. It wasn't all a bed of roses. But overall, I wouldn't have it any other way. I love the Bronx.

Jimmy Owens

Jimmy Owens (1943–) is a world-renowned jazz trumpeter.

My parents got married in 1936 and lived in Harlem until 1939, when they moved to Union Avenue at 163rd Street in the Bronx. I think the address was 975 Union Avenue. They lived there for four years, and in 1943 they moved to 810 East 168th Street, between Union and Prospect Avenues, where I was born.

My father, who worked for the post office, was born in New York City, and my mother was born in Charleston, South Carolina. The musical tradition in my family came from my father's side because he had uncles and cousins who were professional musicians.

My earliest memories go back to 1946, when I was three. My father would always play great music in the house—Duke Ellington or Billie Holiday. We had a huge mirror in our living room, and my father used to pick me up and dance with me in front of this mirror. I loved it. It was so amazing to see my image and my father's image twirling around to the music.

As we got older, there were jazz stations on the radio. My father would listen to *Jumpin' with Symphony Sid* or Mort Fega's show, *Jazz Unlimited*. Just about all of his thirty years in the post office he worked from midnight to eight in the morning. He'd come home, take a nap, and when I came home from school at three he was usually listening to music.

We lived on the top floor of a private house. We had eight rooms for four children. My family lived there until 1965, when they bought another house on Woodcrest Avenue in the Bronx. When I was growing up, there were a few white families, and I also remember when Puerto Rican people started to move in. Most of them were light skinned, so we looked at them as white.

I went to P.S. 99, and in elementary school the main things we did after school were play baseball, and cowboys and Indians, and play in the backyard. We only played street games—skully, stickball, kick-the-can. I always used to play wearing my new shoes, and my mother would get angry with me.

There were gangs around in those days. I remember the Sportsmen and the Seven Crowns, and there were Spanish gangs around Prospect and Longfellow Avenues. My sisters were sometimes friends with Puerto Rican boys, and they'd come back and say, "Such-and-such gang is going to fight such-and-such gang." It was always frightening to me.

In 1955, when I was in sixth grade, the Fordham Baldies decided to attack our neighborhood, and there was a big fight because the gangs from our neighborhood, the Seven Crowns and the Sportsmen, who were always fighting each other, came together to fight this white gang. The fight took place in Crotona Park, and then they came into our neighborhood. I was in the house because I was frightened to death. What our gangs did was take garbage cans and bricks up to the roof, and when the Fordham Baldies arrived, they threw all the stuff down on them. It was a mess. I remember the way the street looked the next day.

Along with gangs, there were lots of people who played the numbers. My father played the numbers, and I used to help out one of the numbers guys who used to give me money. I especially remember a guy named Melvin. He was someone my mother used to get on my father about because Melvin was crazy. He was big and fat, and he always had a brand-new Cadillac. I remember this time when he had a new car, I think it was gray. And he didn't pay someone, so they took garbage cans and a big rock up to the roof and threw them off, and they went right through the roof of his car.

I didn't play an instrument in elementary school because there was no music program. But in the fifth grade I had a friend on the block whose name was Al Henshaw. He'd been in the Korean War, and he had a trumpet I wanted, so he gave it to me. The trumpet was missing a piece, the tuning slide. He had put a piece of rubber tubing there, but the sound was pitiful. He taught me a little bit about playing the trumpet. I could get a sound, and I practiced on it in the fifth and sixth grade.

There were other people on the block who played instruments. I discovered, for example, that a guy named Mr. Sykes, who lived in a building near me, played trumpet. He found out that I played trumpet, invited me up to his room, and showed me things to play.

In 1954 my sisters got a tape recorder. Some local musicians would come over to the house, put on Thelonious Monk, Miles Davis, Gerry Mulligan, and Chet Baker records, and we'd play along with them.

I knew I was going to J.H.S. 40. Mr. Lightner, who was in charge of the music program there, came to P.S. 99 when I was in sixth grade and gave a select group of students a musical aptitude test. I really wanted to get into the special music class, so I was very attentive to everything he said. He'd clap something and then point to someone and say, "Do that back." And I did it, and he'd say, "what's your name?"

When I got to J.H.S. 40, I was put in the special music class right away. This was my homeroom class. Everybody in it was in the special music class, and music was going to be part of the daily curriculum.

We studied music out of a book called *Easy Steps to the Band*. Many years later I did a concert in a private school in Connecticut, and the students were using the same book. "I started with that book," I told them. "That was my first music book." It brought tears to my eyes.

I was in seventh grade when Joe Orange's uncle, the great trombonist J. C. Higginbotham, was playing at the Metropole in Manhattan. Joe and I were too young to get in, but we'd stand outside so we could see the musicians. One of the musicians who worked there was Henry Red Allen. Great jazz trumpet player. He lived at 169th Street and Prospect Avenue, practically around the corner from me. Every day when I was coming home from school, I'd see him standing in front of his building.

After a month, I got the nerve to walk up to him with my trumpet case and say, "Hello, Mr. Allen, my name is James Owens, and I play the trumpet." He became a friend of mine, always talking to me when he saw me come by. He became an important influence on me. My heart used to jump every time I saw him.

Mr. Lightner was the teacher in junior high who had the biggest influence on me. Then in eighth grade a new teacher came. Her name was Edna Smith. She was a professional bass player who worked with a group called the Sweethearts of Rhythm.

When it came time to take the exam for the High School of Music and Art, I said to her, "I want to take that exam." She started asking me questions, and I didn't know the answers. Then she said, "You can't just play good and get in. You have to know music theory." So she started to teach me the scales, the key signatures. I remember she taught me key signatures up to four flats and four sharps.

I'd go to her room after school for individual instruction. On Saturday I'd go and meet her at her house. Sometimes she'd meet me at the beauty parlor because she was there getting her hair done. While she was in the chair, she'd say, "What's the key with one flat? What is that flat? Explain the scale to me."

She'd introduce me to people by saying, "He's going to be a great young musician." I wound up getting into Music and Art thanks to her.

When I graduated from J.H.S. 40, I was playing at various places in the community. But the only places I could perform were the community centers and auditoriums. There was a group of us who were learning how to play, and we'd use these places for jam sessions.

We'd go into Harlem, and there'd be a trumpet player named Faruk Dawud, who wrote the song "Dawud" for his father, Talib Dawud. He played with Dizzy Gillespie. We also heard the pianist Larry Willis and the alto saxophonist Johnny Simon, who were from the Bronx. At P.S. 99 we used the auditorium because there was a guy named Vincent Tibbs, a physical education teacher and a real community person, who presented concerts and took us all under his wing.

I was taken to various places and allowed to sit in with the band. For example, there was a group called the Jazz Art Society that presented concerts at the Club 845 and other places in the Bronx. In 1958 they had a concert at the International Park Inn. The musicians were Kenny Durham, trumpet; Hank Mobley, tenor saxophone; and Curtis Fuller, trombone. My father took me there, and I played with them. Pictures of me at fifteen years old were taken playing with Hank Mobley and Curtis Fuller, and the *Amsterdam News* wrote a story. It was a fantastic experience.

My father also took me to a Sunday matinee at Small's Paradise in Harlem to see Miles Davis. When my father and I walked in, the band was off the stage. We were standing at the bar, and Miles was talking to friends. I went up to the bandstand, which was right near the bar in the middle of the club.

I had read all these stories about Miles Davis being such a nasty son of a bitch. So I was making sure I wasn't going to get too close to his horn. It was resting on the piano. I had never seen a blue trumpet. All of a sudden someone sits down at the piano, and it's Miles. He says to me, "Hey, kid, you play trumpet?" I said, "Yeah." So he's playing some chords on the piano and he stops and says, "Here, play me a tune," and gives me his trumpet. I proceed to take the mouthpiece out, and he said, "What are you going to do? Play without a mouthpiece?" I said, "No, I have my own." I put my mouthpiece in and played "Walkin'," one of his hits. He says, "Sounds good, man. Keep up the work."

At that point all the musicians are coming back to the bandstand, and Miles is standing there with his horn. He says to the pianist Bill Evans, "Hey, Bill, you heard this kid play?" Bill said, "No," and Miles says to me, "Play it again." So I play "Walkin'" again, and the band comes in and joins me. Bill Evans; Paul Chambers, bass; Jimmy Cobb, drums; John Coltrane, tenor saxophone; Cannonball Adderley, alto saxophone. People were going crazy. They loved it.

Then Miles says, "Play another one," so I play "Bags' Groove." That was my introduction to Miles Davis.

We weren't allowed to go to the clubs on Boston Road, but we listened. We'd be sitting outside. I remember going to Freddy's and Sylvia's Blue Morocco. I remember listening to Oliver Beener, a trumpet player, along with George Braithwaite, a saxophonist who's now George Braith, and Arthur Jenkins and Kenny Grant, who played piano.

By the time I was in junior high school, I knew I was going to be a professional musician. I knew when I had to decide between Music and Art, Brooklyn Technical High School, or the High School of Performing Arts.

My mother was very angry with me. My brother-in-law was an electronic engineer working for a big firm and making lots of money, so that was a role model. But music was very special to me. So when I had to make a choice, I selected Music and Art and said I want to be a professional musician.

My mother was not interested in that. She was wary of the sort of culture surrounding professional musicians. Her two nephews, who were a few years older than my sisters, were strung out on drugs in the late 1940s. One of them played trumpet, and the other one played piano. So she was wary about me being a musician because she thought this was something that could happen to me.

She also saw what was happening to people in the neighborhood. She'd say, "Don't hang out with this family because they're strung out."

By the late fifties there was a visible drug problem in Morrisania. It had started in the late forties, and by the late fifties it was hard to avoid knowing about. A lot of players had gotten strung out using a role model like Miles Davis or Billie Holiday and other musicians who were doing drugs. It ruined a lot of lives.

Some of my friends, by the time they got to junior high they'd either dropped out or were put in some kind of juvenile delinquency home. My mother was always warning me, "Don't go and hang out with this person or that person because they're no good, their family's no good." Most of the time she was right.

In my junior year of high school I was in the Newport Youth Band. In the summer of 1960 we played at Newport, and a lot of people who grew up in and around the Bronx were in the band. Larry Morton was an alto saxophonist, and after Music and Art he went to Manhattan School of Music, but he gave up playing and went into teaching. Harry Hall graduated from Music and Art, went to Manhattan School of Music, got terribly strung out, and died of an overdose. Ronnie Cuber is a great baritone saxophonist who's still around.

The drug epidemic in the sixties affected many people who grew up in the Bronx. Joe Orange and I were fortunate because we were so engrossed in music, and we knew what alcohol and drugs would do to us. On our block we had two winos. One was Pop, who lived in a basement right across the street from me, and later he lived at no. 802. And then there was Mrs. Mulligan. She had a broken ankle that was never fixed properly, so she limped and was always drunk. These were the people our parents would bring up. "You want to be like Pop? You want to be like Mrs. Mulligan?" That kept me and my sisters straight.

I was first exposed to Latin music because of my sisters. When I was at J.H.S. 40, they had graduated. They were five and seven years older than me, so they'd gone through their phase of Latin music following Tito Puente, Tito Rodriguez, and Machito. There was somebody named Sugar who was a disk jockey, and my older sister, Yvonne, started to work for him.

He produced a lot of concerts, so she used to get in free and got my other sister, Marcia, in free. They learned how to mambo, and of course my parents were against all of this because we lived on 168th Street and they had to go down below the Prospect Avenue station, which at the time was the Hispanic part of the Bronx. My mother was always saying, "You're going to get pregnant by some of those boys." Fortunately, none of that happened.

I spent my whole last year in high school just studying. My first year and a half of high school were a failure from the standpoint of me as an academic student. My whole concept of life at that time was, "Man, I'm going to be a musician. Why the hell I gotta take biology and English and math?" So biology exams I'd get 23; English exams I'd get 37.

They had a policy at Music and Art that if you were failing academically you wouldn't be kicked out of the school, but if you failed musically, you would be. My music grades were high, but for the first three semesters my academic grades were ridiculous. Then in English the teacher had us read Ralph Waldo Emerson's essay "Self-Reliance." It struck home and turned me completely around. "Speak your latent conviction," he wrote. I started to study and graduated with a good average—82, 83, 84. If I'd continued like before, I'd never have graduated.

At the same time I was studying and practicing every day. Bess Pruitt, who lived in the neighborhood, was always saying, "Whenever it was time for dinner, you'd know because Jimmy would stop practicing."

I graduated from Music and Art, and my intention was to go to Juilliard School of Music. At that time, the tuition was $900 a year. The Manhattan School of Music, where a lot of my friends had gone, was $750 a year. Both of those were out of the picture for my parents. So that summer I practiced eight, nine hours every day. I would go out in the evening and come back to the Bronx and practice.

I'd go to Birdland. I'd go to hear other musicians, but I'd be up at nine o'clock in the morning practicing. If I got in at four in the morning, I'd still be up at nine in the morning practicing. I took the train to Birdland and the Five Spot. By now a lot of the musicians knew me, so if they saw me they'd bring me in with them. I did that for about five months. I really started to improve. But I wasn't taking any gigs. I had a lot people calling me and saying, "Hey, man, can you work with me Monday night at Birdland?" I'd say, "No, I can't. I'm just practicing."

I was studying with a teacher by the name of Carmine Caruso. I used to go down to Fifty-Third Street and Broadway, and I used to pay six dollars a lesson. I was working gigs here and there making a little bit of money. Sometimes I'd get together my money and pay eighteen dollars, so I knew I had three lessons coming up instead of one.

My mother then made me become responsible. "You're going to have to be responsible sometime," she said. "You're going to have a family to support. You're never going to make any money playing this music. You have to get a job." I said, "I'm not responsible? I practice every day, all day long."

Anyway, she made me look for a job. I'd go down to the employment agencies and fill out cards and then go to the movies down on Forty-Second Street. Finally, after about five months—this must have been 1961—she got me a job at Lincoln Hospital, where she worked in the clerical office.

She found out that somebody had left for the military. This guy was called a stationery clerk, and he worked in a room with all these paper supplies. I worked real hard for two weeks out of the month taking requisitions, ordering the stuff, and distributing it. The rest of the time I'd close my door, lock it with a big skeleton key, and practice. I'd be in there practicing, and someone would knock on the door. I'd open the door, and they'd say, "Here's the requisition. I need this stuff."

I worked at that job for a year and three months. Only time in my life I've ever worked outside of music. I saved my money to go to Juilliard, and I studied privately with Carmine Caruso, and I saved a good bit of money. I think my take-home pay was like $99.68 every two weeks. I started to work a few gigs here and there. Then I quit and was out of work for about two days when Slide Hampton, who I knew, called me. He lived in the Bronx around the corner from 160th Street.

We went down to Greenville, North Carolina, and made $300. We played the concert, turned around, and drove right back to New York, but that was more money than I had made in a whole month. And from that point on I practiced more and started to work more. I also played in a lot of rehearsal bands. By now I'm a very experienced reader of music. I can read anything you put in front of me. I can read any trombone music and transpose it.

It was all word of mouth. Musicians who like the way you play, they'd call you for a gig. The first couple of gigs that I worked, I worked with the guitarist Sal Salvador. I wrote arrangements for his big band and started to work with more people. Monday night at Birdland, the Village Gate. I also got rock and roll gigs. Many times Joe Orange had a gig, and he'd say, "I know a trumpet player." And they'd say, "Well, bring him."

I worked with Slide Hampton and his ten-piece band, and we worked pretty regularly for seven or eight months. By now it's 1962, 1963, and we went to Virginia Beach and integrated the beach. Two days before they'd passed an ordinance saying that black people could go on the beach, but there were no black people going on the beach. We didn't know this. It was an integrated band, ten people, and I'm sure we caused a ruckus.

After Slide Hampton I worked with Lionel Hampton, and after a few months he needed another trombonist. I said, "I got a friend," and Joe got the gig. I stayed with Lionel Hampton about a year, wrote music for him, and by this time I'm getting better known. At the end of 1963 I started to work with the saxophonist Hank Crawford, and I worked with him for awhile.

We worked out of Mobile, Alabama, for three months, and we had a station wagon. There were nine of us in the band, so there were three seats up front, three seats in the middle, and three seats facing the back. We pulled a U-Haul trailer that was wider than the car. The people who sat in the back seat had to be the smallest people in the band. I was one of the smallest people. I sat in the back, and I could not see beyond this U-Haul trailer.

I think there were about eight guns in this band, or maybe it was eleven guns. Anyway, it was a ridiculous amount of guns. Plus we had New York license plates. So we decided that if we were ever stopped by these cracker cops, we'd have to kill them to get out of this. Fortunately we never had problems, but for those months we worked in Alabama, Mississippi, Florida, and South Carolina, it was very heavy.

Later I went with Charles Mingus. The Mingus experience was really wonderful. We worked at Birdland for two weeks. One week beside Billy Taylor and his trio, which was Earl May, bass; and Grady Tate, drums. Then the next week it was beside John Coltrane's great quartet.

From there I started to work with Herbie Mann. He was trying to do something like Eddie Palmieri was doing, so he had two trombones, and I managed to get Joe on the gig. We went to Japan, and I started to record with Herbie, and our first gig was one where he hired Oliver Nelson to write music for two trombones, trumpet, a horn, and Herbie playing flute. Oliver Nelson really liked my playing and would call me for concerts, recording sessions, commercial jingles, things like that.

After Herbie Mann I decided to give up the road because I'd gotten married. Now it's 1966. A dear friend of mine, Garnett Brown, a trombonist, introduced me to his wife, Hannah. Garnett said, "Hey, man, Hannah has somebody she'd like to introduce you to." So she introduced me to this lady. Her name was Lola Clark, and we liked each other. We started to make a thing of it, but I was still going out on the road. I was working with Hank Crawford at that time, and that's when we got married, in 1965.

At that point Lola was living at Nineteenth Street and Park Avenue South with her daughter, who was eleven, and I moved into her place. I had lived away from the Bronx only for a week or two here and there. I'd have this girlfriend and that girlfriend, and then we'd break up, and I'd have to move back to the Bronx to my parents' house. I never moved my stuff out, but this time I moved my stuff out of the Bronx for good.

After I left for Manhattan and my parents moved to the Yankee Stadium area, I went back to 168th Street a few times. One time was in 1988. I went back with my sister Marcia, who was born in 1939. We took my father in the car, and we went to the places we'd all been born: my older sister, Yvonne, in Harlem, then where my parents lived when they moved to the Bronx on Union Avenue and 163rd Street, and then 168th Street, where I was born.

I went back at that time to visit Bess Pruitt. I'd stayed in contact with her because she had a management agency, and I knew some of the people she managed. My sister is a wheeler dealer, and she got Bess Pruitt to manage me. She said to her, "Jimmy's great!" And we worked together for a long time. But I had no friends in the Bronx. All my friends had moved, died, or were in jail.

In 1966 I decided to give up the road and stay in New York. In 1967 we had our first child, a daughter. I'm working studio gigs. I'm busy making money in New York. In 1968 I work with Duke Ellington, Count Basie, and Max Roach.

In 1969, Billy Taylor called me to work with him on the David Frost television show. I stayed on that show until 1972, making $55,000 a year. I was also still very busy working as Jimmy Owens, the jazz trumpet player. I was making well over $100,000 a year. In 1967 I also started to do more writing, and I was with the Metropole Orchestra. I wrote my first piece for them in 1968 and for the next twenty-five years worked with them and with other radio orchestras in New York.

In 1967 I started to get into education. Chris White, the bass player who was working with me, started something called Rhythm Associates. It started out teaching rhythm players how to play—drummers, bass players, pianists. He had Kenny Barron teaching piano; he had Rudy Collins teaching drums. That was the rhythm section of Dizzy Gillespie's band in the early sixties. Then he added horns, and I became the person who would teach trumpet, and Kenny Barron's brother taught saxophone.

That experience was very rewarding. It brought back so many memories of all of the people who helped me, like Donald Byrd and Edna Smith and all of the musicians. People would help me when I'd go to them and ask them questions—J. J. Johnson, Oliver Nelson, Ernie Wilkins, Thad Jones, you name it. People who I sat in the same trumpet section with, like Clark Terry, Ernie Royal, and Jimmy Nottingham. And a lot of these people have some history of staying in the Bronx, so it was rewarding for me to remember what they'd given me free of charge.

We had another group called the New York Jazz Sextet. It was Roland Hanna, piano; Ron Carter, bass; Billy Carver on the drums; Tom McIntosh, trombone; originally Benny Goldstein, tenor saxophone; and me, trumpet. When Benny Goldstein left to go to California, we replaced him with Hubert Laws, who played tenor saxophone. We didn't play clubs. We only played concerts. This was 1968.

When the New York Jazz Sextet broke up in 1969, I took the nucleus of that group, which was Billy Carver, added Kenny Barron and Chris White, and started to work as Jimmy Owens Plus. Sometimes we'd fly to Europe to do a concert. I started to write more music for orchestra and big band and recorded it. I started to perform more in colleges and do workshops in colleges all over the United States.

Basically, that's how I make my living now. I perform in concerts, do workshops and concerts in colleges and universities all over the world, and occasionally tour with my group. I've done State Department tours, North Africa, the Middle East, and I've done lots of concerts in South America and Central America.

During the sixties I also started to teach. I taught at Old Westbury out on Long Island, at Queensborough Community College, and starting in 1990 at the New School. I teach just one day a week, on Wednesday. I do concerts, and I'm back by Wednesday.

I have two children, thirty-eight and thirty-three. I was married for twenty-six years. I've been married for six years to my new wife, Stephanie. I travel all over the world. For the last ten years I've done only what I want to do, what I like to do. I've had places to live in Italy and Paris. We go to our place and relax in the summertime or wintertime. I like my life.

Andrea Ramsey

Andrea Ramsey (1943–) worked for many years as an art therapist.

My maternal grandparents, Edith Nurse Prout and Rigaude Placide Prout, who were from Barbados, moved to the Bronx in the late 1950s. They were living on the Upper West Side in the nineties, and then they moved to 974 Union Avenue between 163rd and 165th Streets. He was a mailman, she was a housewife, and they had two daughters, Margery and Gloria, who was my mother.

My parents were both Caribbean, and a lot of their friends from the Caribbean were moving to the Bronx. Rents were a little cheaper than in Harlem, and the apartments were nicer. After living for a little while in a walkup, they moved to 1105 Tinton Avenue between 166th Street and Home Street.

My father's family was from Antigua, my mother's family was from Barbados, and the sense of Caribbean identity was strong on both sides. It didn't matter what island you were from. But my maternal grandfather was pretty unusual because he had friends from every ethnic group imaginable. He had Irish friends; he had Jewish friends; he belonged to the Civil Defense League, so you know there was a Mr. Friedberg or a Mr. Sullivan there. He didn't really stick to Caribbeans.

He did play cricket, however, so he had a lot of Caribbean friends through that. He played at both Randall's Island and Van Cortlandt Park. Although I went to the games, I never learned the rules. But I did like the coconut drops they sold there. They were made of pure sugar and coconut. They just kind of mixed it all together, and then the mixture got hard.

Hundreds of people would come to these matches, and the men all wore white uniforms. They still play on Sundays up in Van Cortlandt Park. I still see them there in their white outfits.

When we moved to the Bronx, we started going to St. Augustine's Presbyterian Church, so we were very involved with Reverend Hawkins and the whole St. Augustine's community.

It was an incredibly vibrant scene. If you didn't get to church early, you couldn't get a seat. The place was packed. And in addition to the Sunday services, they had all types of activities. They had Girl Scout troops, they had Boy Scout troops, they had everything imaginable. They had roller skating, church plays. It was the community's social life in that neighborhood.

When I was nine or ten, I went to their camp for the first time. It was called Camp Ohado, and it was up in the Catskills, I think. It was pretty rugged. I mean, it was an old farmhouse. I think they used chicken coops for bunks. The girls' dorm was like a barn, and it was pretty rustic. I also remember loads of mosquitoes. There was a swamplike lake to swim in, and we did arts and crafts. It wasn't what camp is like now. I don't think kids today would really want to go to this camp.

My elementary school was P.S. 23 on East 165th Street between Union and Tinton. The students were mostly black with a few Latinos and a few whites. Most of the teachers were Irish and Jewish, but there were a few black teachers.

Culturally we got a very rich African American sense of who we were. We always sang the Negro national anthem, and this was even in classes with white teachers. We also had music appreciation. I listened to classical music, and to this day I know tunes by Offenbach. I also remember that Jay Silverheels, the actor who played Tonto on *The Lone Ranger,* came to school and taught us about Native American folk tales.

Students were tracked by ability level. They had SP classes for kids who were more advanced and could do two grades in one, so they could graduate a little earlier. My sister was in the SP class, and so was Augusta Kappner, who later became president of Bank Street College of Education.

The community itself was very vibrant, with a mixture of immigrants from the Caribbean and migrants from the South. People didn't visit each others' houses, but we knew each other just from being on the street. In those days there were no play dates or anything like that. You just went out and played, and you knew all the kids in the neighborhood, and all the kids and all the families knew you.

There wasn't a lot of adult supervision. It was mostly from the window where my grandmother would look out at us. When the sun went down, we came upstairs, where we'd sit on the fire escape and watch other kids outside.

Most of my earlier years were spent on Union Avenue, where my maternal grandparents lived. My parents worked, so during the week I stayed with them.

My mother was an office assistant. First she worked for the tax department, and then she worked at Hunter College. My father was manager of a vegetable store in Harlem, and then he became part owner of Saxon Beer and Soda, a beer and soda distributor on Intervale Avenue.

My maternal grandfather was politically sophisticated. He talked politics at the dinner table, and he belonged to the Civil Defense League and a lot of organizations, including, of course, cricket clubs, so there was a lot of political conversation. From my grandmother too. She read three newspapers every day even though she never got a high school diploma because when she came here she was fourteen and had to work.

There was a lot of encouragement of academic achievement, and we were also encouraged to explore the arts. We took dancing lessons. I started music lessons, too, but unfortunately the cousin who was giving me the lessons, her house caught on fire and she moved uptown. I learned where middle C was, and that was about as good as it got. For dance, my sister and I went to a dancing school near the Bronx Zoo. And before that, when I was three or four, I went to the Katherine Dunham School of Dance. But I wasn't meant to be a dancer. I was forced to put on a costume and jump on the stage, which I didn't do very well.

Reading was also an important part of my childhood. My parents enrolled me in kindergarten when I was four, but my grandmother had read with me so much that I had become a fluent reader, and so the school put me in first grade instead. My family didn't complain because my grandmother had my sister and my younger cousin to take care of at home, so they decided to leave me in first grade because the class went all day. I could keep up with the work, but developmentally I was just a baby. I always felt a little backwards because I was much younger than all the other kids in class.

In the summer we used to go to Rockaway Beach, where we usually stayed with my grandmother. There were a lot of other grandmothers, most of them of Caribbean descent. The Weeks family, who also came from the Caribbean, had two houses on Beach 77th Street, and they rented rooms. In one house, families shared everything. You had to make up a schedule showing when you would cook, when you would take a shower. The other house was for the more affluent people, and she would cook for them. If I went with my mother, we would stay on that side because my mother wasn't able to cook. When I went with my grandmother, we stayed on the other side because she cooked.

Every Wednesday there were fireworks. There was a Jewish couple who owned a candy store that sold ice cream, so on the way back we'd get ice cream. Plus we collected shells, which we painted and sold. We made lemonade. If you walked up to Beach 99th, it was Rockaway Playland. We went in the water every day and stayed the whole day. Sometimes I go to the beaches now, and the waves are so cold I can't imagine how I stood in them.

The best thing I remember about Rockaway is that they had this Jewish bakery where they made cherry cheese knishes. We used to get them hot, and they were delicious. I've been looking for cherry cheese knishes ever since.

When I was growing up, you always heard groups of guys singing in the neighborhood. Every guy had a group, and so did the girls. It wasn't about money. It just seems like people sang because people wanted to sing. I remember Arthur Crier, who lived in our building, singing all the time. I was good friends with his sister Shirley, who used to sing too, and so did her sister Linda. Her mother was a pianist at St. Augustine's at one time, so I think her family was musically inclined.

Once Arthur got popular there was more of a push to make a record. But it wasn't like now where everyone wants to be a rapper.

I went to Olinville Junior High School, which is on 216th Street. My mother had a friend named Mr. Kelly who she worked with at Hunter College and who lived up there, so I used his address to get in. From there I went to Evander Childs.

When I was eleven or twelve, my friends and I formed a club. We started out as the Polly Pigtails. I'd read an article that said this was a club for young white girls, but what did we know? So we named ourselves the Black Polly Pigtails. Then when we went to junior high we became the Lace Angeliques. The club consisted of me, my sister Tony, Shirley, Marie Mackenzie, Linda Hill, my friend Lana Hinds, and later Joyce Hansen, who became a well-known children's book author.

We were very civic minded. We'd have raffles where we'd get the merchants in the neighborhood to donate things. Or we'd go door to door and ask people to donate things, and with the money we raised we'd take neighborhood kids to the zoo, kids who had never been to the zoo. We did a lot of very nice things.

We once threw a party on Belmont Avenue, off Tremont, where Joyce Hansen's family lived. In those days young girls weren't allowed to go out late at night. The party wasn't late, just from eight to twelve, but no girls came. So we had about fifty boys in Joyce's mother's basement. It was a great fiasco. We didn't mind because we had all the boys. But Joyce's mother was a little appalled.

I have only a vague recollection of racial tension in the neighborhood, but there definitely were gangs. I never saw any real gang warfare, but I remember hearing about the Seven Crowns. And I remember a young man named Carl who was killed in front of a drugstore on 163rd and Union. They said it was gang related, though I didn't know who the other gang was. When I went to Evander, we were always afraid of the Fordham Baldies, a big Italian gang.

After high school I went to Fashion Institute of Technology, where I studied textile designing. I worked in the industry for a little while, and then in 1962, when I was eighteen, I got married.

I met my husband through a friend named Richard Powell, who was a musician. He had a band, and he invited a group of my friends to hear them practice in his basement on Crotona Avenue. My future husband was a trumpet or saxophone player. I don't think either of our families were too thrilled about the idea because I was so young.

When we were first married, we lived on Franklin Avenue, and my daughter was born a year later. But my husband was in the Air Force, and so we moved around a lot—to San Angelo, Texas, then Anchorage, Alaska, and then Tucson, Arizona. In the four years he was in the service we lived in three different places. When we came back to the Bronx, we lived on Crotona Avenue and then Shakespeare Avenue, and finally we moved to Tracey Towers.

By the time we got married, the neighborhood where I grew up had already begun to change. I first became aware of heroin when I was in junior high. I saw a lot of guys I'd gone to elementary school with, and they were already drug addicts. You'd see them nodding or looking disheveled, and they'd stopped going to school. Later I remember seeing girls, but those days it was mostly the guys.

It was a big problem because the guys would rob to get drugs, and people stopped leaving their doors unlocked. There had always been numbers in the neighborhood, but the drugs were something completely different.

There really wasn't any way to explain the heroin plague. People just accepted the situation and hoped that they didn't get robbed and that their children didn't become strung out. But this didn't affect my coming home late at night or saying I'm not going to walk home from the subway at eleven or anything like that.

I remember going to a dance at FIT. I came home about two in the morning, got off the subway, and walked down Prospect Avenue going to no. 1105. This man stopped me in the rain and said, "Are you Butler's daughter?" I said, "Yeah." And he said, "My name is Lip, and don't ever be afraid to walk down these streets."

Gangs were scary, but I didn't see the gangs. The drugs I saw. A lot of kids on my block became involved, and their lives just went down the tubes.

And it wasn't just kids in the lower academic tracks. I remember one of the Stover boys. I think he was the first person on Tinton Avenue to go away to college, and to find out he was doing drugs was mind boggling. Plus he came from a two-parent home. I guess at that age people thought drugs were cool, hip, not realizing the extent to which they'd get hooked on heroin. And I think that's what happened. Kids were experimenting like kids do, and the next thing you knew they had a habit.

By the 1980s, when my husband and I were living on Shakespeare Avenue, most people who had lived in Morrisania had already left the area. Occasionally, I'd go back when they had the Old Timers' reunion. But it was sad because so few people from my generation seemed to have made it through. A lot of them were gone. Every time I'd asked about someone, they'd say, "Oh, he died, and he died." It was depressing. Drugs really played a big part in accounting for people not living out their lives.

When I go back to the area today, I feel very sad because it doesn't look like the same place. If you were to put me on Prospect Avenue and turn me around, I probably wouldn't know where the heck I was. It's nice to see St. Anthony's and St. Augustine's and a few of the buildings. But my grandmother's building on Union Avenue, that's gone. That whole side of Union Avenue, nothing is there. They just have senior citizens' housing and a parking lot. They changed the whole structure of the neighborhood when they put up those little townhouses.

When I lived there, people stayed out a lot, especially kids. Any time you had the opportunity to be outside, you were. A lot of times you went up to Crotona Pool. They had a night pool, so you could go in the evening. People didn't worry so much about drowning back then. They had lifeguards, but they didn't worry that you were going to drown.

I'm still in touch with my childhood friends. We try to get together every once in a while. Joyce lives in Columbia, South Carolina, and Shirley moved up to the boondocks, so it's hard for us to get together, but we e-mail and keep in contact and let each other know what's going on. Marie McKenzie lives in New Jersey, but she came down, and we went to see the wrestler Dustin Rhodes.

My daughter doesn't have that. She doesn't have that core of friends she grew up with.

I sometimes think about what created this camaraderie. When I lived in 1105 Tinton Avenue, it was a double-courtyard building, and I knew every single person, and every single person knew me. That doesn't happen anymore. If you know the people who live on your floor, you're lucky. We knew everybody, and everybody knew you. When you had a friend, it was for life. My aunt still has the same friends she had when she was growing up, at least the ones who are left. She's eighty-five, but they call and keep in contact.

Looking back at the positive years in Morrisania, before the drugs hit, when you're living in such a period, you don't think of it as so positive because at the time it wasn't anything special. But when you see what life is like now, you say, "Hey, that wasn't so bad." There were a lot of different kinds of people in the neighborhood. People were alcoholics; people were gay. The two women who lived below us were gay, and nobody ever said anything. There wasn't much focus on trying to label people.

But there was also some social consciousness in the community. Reverend Hawkins of St. Augustine's was always having fundraisers for different causes. He was very outspoken, and it was a time when people needed that kind of leadership.

Plus most people were generous. They really had to help each other to survive. There were people who were on home relief, but they were never made to feel bad about it. It wasn't a perfect world, far from it, but it left me with a feeling that was good, and I think that's what a lot of people remember.

You can talk about all the bad things; you can talk about all of the horror stories. But when you go back in your memory, you try and remember good things. And there were enough of those things to realize that it was not just one person's fantasy. Those good things were real.

Daphne Moss

Daphne Moss (1947–) has worked as a registered nurse, a teacher, and a school administrator.

My parents both came from Jamaica, but they met in the United States. I think they started out in Harlem, but after they got married they lived in different places. The story goes that it was easier to move to a new apartment than to paint the one you had. They lived in several apartments in the Prospect Avenue area in the Bronx, and they ended up on Simpson Street, which is where I was born.

I think that my father was an elevator operator, and after mechanization came in he became a night watchman on one of the Hudson railroad lines. My mother had seven children, of which I was the youngest, and I think she didn't start working until I started school. She worked as a domestic, doing housework and cooking. No one ever taught her to cook. She just figured it out.

We were also superintendents in a five-story walkup on Simpson Street. We lived in the basement, and for a little girl the window ledges seemed very high. Our building faced the no. 2 and 5 trains, which went right past our house.

We were the only Jamaicans on our block, which was changing from Irish and Jewish. There was one African American super, but the vast number of people who were moving in were Puerto Rican. No one knew what a Jamaican was.

In the beginning, all of my friends were Puerto Rican except for one

Jewish girl. From her I learned about matzo, some Jewish culture, and the language. I think that our landlord, Mr. Kramer, was also Jewish. My school, P.S. 20, was largely white with a few Puerto Ricans and one or two blacks.

My father died in 1954, when I was seven. My mom got very little help from her family, but there were a few aunts who did help out. And a great-aunt had sponsored my mother when she came here from Jamaica. That's how I learned about show money, that you had to have that $50 to get off Ellis Island. You couldn't get off Ellis Island without show money, an address, and proof of health.

My mother never traveled back to Jamaica. It was as though she had cut her ties with the country. However, my father talked about the country. Just little stories that I can remember, but I felt his affection for the place.

After my father died, we started going to St. Ann's Episcopal Church on St. Ann's Avenue. My mother joined the altar guild, so she was the person who set up the altar and put up the flowers, and she got very involved with the church. This was good for her, I think, being a single woman with all these kids and the grandchildren starting to come.

I, being the youngest, had no choice about going to church. The others could say no, but I had to go. I joined the choir, and I also had to go to the Girls' Friendly Society.

There was a large Jamaican group in the church. But on my block, which was becoming predominantly Puerto Rican, I had a hard time. First of all, I wasn't petite. You had all these tiny little girls who were Puerto Rican, and I was five-foot-seven and already in the sixth grade. So I knew I was not one of the Puerto Ricans, but I think people may have looked at me and thought I was. I remember people saying, "Where are you from?" and I'd say, "From Jamaica." They'd say, "Where's that?" And I'd say, "The West Indies." I'd have to explain that Jamaica was an island in the Caribbean and that it was even bigger than Puerto Rico.

I didn't identify with Puerto Ricans, but there wasn't really anyone else to identify with. All my friends during adolescence were Puerto Rican, what I describe as five-four, little noses, straight black hair, cute. I just didn't fit.

On my block there were Puerto Ricans who were significantly darker than me. There were Puerto Ricans of all colors. My friends tried to get me to learn Spanish. I could understand it, but I really couldn't speak it. I have a sister who was fluent in Spanish. But I was very hesitant. I don't think I spoke Spanish until I became a nurse and I had to speak to a patient. Then I began to lose my inhibitions.

The culture of the people around me was mostly Latino. We didn't use the term Bootarican to describe ourselves. I don't think people identified me as black. I was looked at more as Caribbean or as the strange one who didn't quite fit in. I wasn't seen as African American.

When it came to my social life in those years, my mom set certain boundaries. I could go to Hunts Point Palace and Club Cubano. She wasn't letting me go to the Palladium or even downtown Latin spots because I was too young. All of my friends were beginning to go, but I was the youngest, so I couldn't. I could do things in the Bronx, however, and we'd go to parties every Saturday.

I learned to dance salsa in the hallway of my building. To this day I can close my eyes and do it. I have a friend whose son is in Iraq right now. When he got married last year and all kinds of music were played at the wedding, she and I got up and danced exactly the way we danced forty years ago.

I had a good elementary school experience and very good teachers. The classes were organized by reading levels, and because I was in the class with the top reading level, I had the best teachers. The male teachers took care of the bad classes with all the boys who wouldn't obey. In terms of its racial mix, I think the school was probably beginning to turn, but because I was in the top class, we still had a few Irish and Jewish kids.

After elementary school I went to the junior high on Stebbins Avenue, where I was in the SP—"special progress"—class, and you did seventh and eighth grade in one year.

As for how my teachers saw me, in elementary school I was known as one of the Moss children. When I left the sixth grade, the principal congratulated my mother and thanked her because I was the last of the Moss children. We were known in the school. We were known as achievers.

Once I started high school, once you walked from Simpson Street toward Morris High School, the population was definitely African American. For the first time I saw this vast number of tall men.

When I went to Morris High School, which was from 1961 to 1964, it had a bad reputation. And it wasn't even the school I wanted to go to. What happened was that they introduced this honors school that was pulling some students from around the city with higher reading levels.

By high school I'd begun to listen to rock and roll and then salsa on the radio. The new music was the pachanga, which changed everything; it was a new beat for young people. I remember going to these parties with my Puerto Rican friends, and they played music from the Isley Brothers and Jackie Wilson, and then they'd throw on some Latin music.

I also remember a lot of doo-wop. All the guys were harmonizing in the hallways and on the street corners. The Puerto Rican guys, everyone. Everybody knew those songs.

And everyone on the block listened to Motown when Motown arrived in the early sixties. But even though you had Motown, you were still listening to Elvis Presley. The Beatles were beginning to filter in at this time too. So there was a really wide range of music. Symphony Sid, the disk jockey, played jazz, Latin, rock and roll, everything.

I heard Tito Puente in person at the International, a club on Westchester Avenue near Intervale that was once called the Tropicana, and saw him more than once. I was thirteen, borrowing my sister Valerie's dresses and going to these clubs because I was tall, and I could pass for an adult and get in.

To hear Tito Puente in person was phenomenal. I can hear the timbales in my head at this moment. After church on Sundays I used to have lunch, change my clothes, and go to the International from three to eight and dance.

I also heard the trombonist Barry Rogers and Mongo Santamaria. The big thing was to hear Mongo and Puente at the same place, and I did at the Hunts Point Palace. I heard all of them for maybe two dollars on a Sunday afternoon.

I remember the names of some of the dances we did, like the Mashed Potato and Mickey's Monkey. We used to dance in the middle of the street. It would be a Saturday night, the weather was hot, and somebody was blasting some music. They called me the Big White Lady. There were a couple of guys who would tease me. "Here comes Ines's friend, the big white lady!"

These were black guys. So in the Puerto Rican world I wasn't really Puerto Rican, and in the black world I wasn't really black.

I was too young to absorb what was going on in the country in terms of racial politics and civil rights, but I was getting very frightened by the drugs coming into the neighborhood. By now it was no longer pot; it was heroin. I was told by one of the guys on the block that by the end of the year everybody was going to be strung out.

I didn't know that my first boyfriend was into the drug culture. Someone said he was skin popping, which I later found out was shooting heroin into your skin. He became a drug addict, and many years later he died from an overdose. He'd been an altar boy at St. Andrew's. His nickname was Churchy, and he went to church regularly, but that couldn't save him from heroin.

I don't know what made this drug so powerful and so popular with the guys at that point, but looking back I think it was a way to undermine other groups. We had social clubs. Prospect Avenue might have been the Knights. We were the Crowns. The girls had their own little club. We had parties and dances on Saturdays, and we hung out together.

And guys would meet other guys, so sometimes there were fights. It was fistfights, trashcan covers, chains. There were no guns at this time, but it felt like the introduction of drugs was undermining the community. That was really the beginning of the end. I saw guys get sent to jail and back to Puerto Rico. Guys were also starting to be drafted because of Vietnam.

I knew quite a few people who ended up going. Some were drafted, but others couldn't be drafted because of heroin. Some went to Vietnam and came back strung out.

I'd grown up in a pretty safe and secure environment, so it was devastating to see my block destroyed. And at this point my family pulled out. I was the last of seven, so my older siblings saw all of this. They saw the neighborhood changing, and they pulled me and my mom out. By this point I was the only one home.

We ended up in the North Bronx, which by then was all Jamaican. But my family didn't think of itself as particularly Jamaican. I had a brown-skinned sister, but I also had blonde and blue-eyed sisters. I have two married sisters, one married to a Puerto Rican and the other married to a Dominican. My brother's second wife was of German descent, and another brother's wife is Irish. So we don't really fit into a category because we have so many offshoots.

I remember watching the news about the civil rights movement and all that film from the South showing those dogs in Birmingham. You're watching Martin Luther King and yet I'm not feeling him because I couldn't turn the other cheek. I'm not from the South. I couldn't handle it. I couldn't be passive like that. I wasn't mature enough to even be able to appreciate how much restraint it took. It wasn't until Malcolm came along that I began to understand these issues better. I heard of him through a boyfriend who had gone to jail. That was Churchy. He was the first person who introduced me to the whole concept of the Muslims. The Muslims believed that the white man was the devil, a concept I rejected because I thought it was absolutely ridiculous. But later on, when I took black history courses and started learning about Africa and the slave trade, I realized where he was coming from with that little simple phrase.

My mother hated Churchy. Everybody hated him. They probably saw what I refused to see at that time. I couldn't bring him home. He was just an infatuation.

By my later teens we'd moved to the Northeast Bronx. I'd graduated from high school and was working for the telephone company.

I have a sister who's a nurse. She's ten years older than me, so I was eight and she was eighteen when she was a nursing school student. She'd bring home stories from Bellevue Hospital and the tough times she'd had as a nursing school student. But she said to me, if you want to be independent, one of the best things you can do for yourself is to become a nurse. So I decided to go to nursing school, and I went to Bellevue, just like my sister did.

When my mother and I lived in the Northeast Bronx, we were in a fifth-floor walkup on 221st Street off Bronxwood Avenue. The neighborhood was predominantly black middle class, but it had a Caribbean flavor, and there were some people who had moved straight from Jamaica. This was in the mid-sixties, right after immigration laws changed, and so there was this huge influx.

Then Parkchester opened up. Parkchester had been strictly Jewish and Irish, but the civil rights laws regarding housing changed, and so my mother could live in an elevator building.

I always thought there was animosity between the African Americans who had been in the Bronx and the new arrival of Caribbean immigrants. And there was always an arrogance from the Jamaicans, from the new Jamaicans and even the old Jamaicans. They were arrogant about their superiority over African Americans.

I think it's just like what happens now, how African Americans are regarded as being lazy, shiftless people who don't know the history, who don't understand the struggle. It took me many years and African

American history courses to understand that. I came up with a feeling of coming from a distinctive land mass and calling it your home, something that gives you a sense of belonging that African Americans do not have. At least that's my theory.

And I felt this even though my family didn't go back to Jamaica, even though my father, who identified so much with Jamaica, died at an early age. I still got that sense of knowing that I was different from African Americans. It was just something I knew.

Colin Powell is my second cousin. When I was growing up, my mother was close to his father, Luther. They were cousins, and I remember visiting the family. They lived on Kelly Street, and later they moved to a house in Queens.

I remember a picture being taken of this whole crowd of family on the couch. I was probably nine or ten. But my real memory of Colin Powell was at my older sister's wedding. Because my mother was close to Colin's father, he helped my mother a lot. There was a lot of prejudice and looking down on my mother because she had these seven kids. When my father passed there was a struggle, and I remember it was Uncle Luther who helped out.

Two years ago I went to the wake for Colin's aunt with my sister Jean, who was her goddaughter. We get to the church, and there's all these Secret Service people. We're laughing about the Secret Service women and wondering if they're going to stop us.

After moving to Parkchester, I went back to visit Simpson Street, and it was traumatic. My building was gone. The stoop, which looked enormous and which was where we all congregated and looked for everybody, is now the size of a table.

We were three buildings down from the Forty-First Precinct, which was known as Fort Apache. As a little girl I spent a lot of summers running into the precinct because it was cool. We would just to walk past the big desk, with all the policemen there. Then I found out that they were the enemy.

Here's what happened. I was about eleven, and we were in the schoolyard. A little white girl had been picked on by some kids. Her pinafore or something had been pulled down, and they were looking for the people who raped her. The Forty-First Precinct was like my backyard, my home, and I don't remember why, but we were walking on the wall surrounding the building. We used to do this just because it was a challenge. It was something to do in the summer, like climbing the most trees or whatever.

On the way back I saw everybody running, and I didn't know what was going on. A big tall policeman took me in the precinct house. He started yelling, and I was taken to the interrogation room, and I instinctively lied to him. I told him my name was Carmen Rivera and that I lived at 933 Tiffany Street, apartment whatever, phone number is da-da-da.

At one point he said, "I'm going to call your mother." He stood up, and I went to touch him. He said, "Get your piece of shit hands"—or something like that—"off of me." It was such a horrible feeling because up until then the policemen had always been my friends.

I was picked up because I was in the right spot at the right time. They finally let me go, and there was a crowd outside. Some of the kids had heard that "Da-pha-ne"—they could never say my name right— was in the precinct. I came out and walked by everyone like I'm fine. And after I got to my apartment building, I burst into tears and told my mother what had happened. She said, "Oh, stop it, that's silliness." She didn't think she should have been outraged by the fact that I had been pulled into the precinct.

When I left nursing school they told us that a bachelor's degree was going to be essential. I finished Bellevue in June of 1969, and that September I registered at Hunter College. It was there that I met Dr. Rodriguez-Abad, a professor who taught me about Vietnam and South Africa. That was my real introduction to activism, and I remember signing a zillion petitions against the war.

I also remember walking to Hunter College one day, and there was this immense rally going on with people carrying pig heads on sticks. I was wearing red, white, and blue pinstriped bellbottoms and a little top. I walked in and heard that the rally was protesting the firing of Dr. Rodriguez-Abad. I couldn't believe he was going to be fired after he opened up my whole world.

The protesters marched into the president's office. They just walked in and sat down. I sat there, and then I said to myself: "What the hell are you doing here? You just got your state board license as a registered professional nurse, and you better get out of here." So I got up and left, and it's a good thing I did because the police came, and I would have lost my license.

Dr. Rodriguez-Abad awakened so much in me. Then I was able to take classes with John Henrik Clark, and I eventually met Yosef Ben-Jochannan—Dr. Ben.

I took classes with him and became very sensitive to the whole subject of Africa.

I remember one class I took on Malcolm X. Dr. Ben made a study of his speeches, his rhetoric, how he spoke, how he was able to empower the crowd and make people laugh at their own weaknesses. This made me reflect on my experience growing up, and I was able to identify with Malcolm X. I didn't really know how I fit in. John Henrik Clark helped me to accept my identity as an African. He gave me an assignment on the East African slave trade. That was a challenge, and it helped me form my own identity and get comfortable with myself.

After Hunter I went to Fordham. I majored in social sciences, and then I got a master's degree in health education. But it wasn't my goal to go into the school system and teach science and health education. What happened was this. I was working as a nurse, and my sister Valerie said to me, "Why don't you take the test to teach nursing?"

And I did. I taught nursing for a while, stopped, and they begged me to come back in 1980 when my son was born. I got a call from a principal who said, "I understand you've passed the nursing exam to teach nursing. I need you as of yesterday."

This school was Benjamin Franklin High School in East Harlem. Having been away from the mixture of the African American and Latino community, I got smacked with it again. I saw the kids and how they interacted with each other and the blending of the two cultures, and I was amazed. This was the eighties, the time of early hip-hop, a whole other generation.

I was very aware of hip-hop. My stepson was writing hip-hop sitting on my couch every day. He's thirty-eight, so in 1980 he was seventeen. His current name is Shaheim Johnson, and he was in the first group of Edenwald writers.

At Benjamin Franklin I taught nursing, and in 1995 I moved into administration. When Benjamin Franklin closed, I went to the North Bronx, to Evander Childs, where I had a great mentor who was African American. She really taught me how to teach, and I kept her program going. She taught at the nursing program first, and then I took it over. Her name was Rhynita Coram. She's still alive, a churchgoing woman in Harlem.

When I was teaching at Benjamin Franklin, most of my students were African American. The kids from the community knew it wasn't a good school, so their parents sent them elsewhere, but a lot of kids had nowhere else to go. And even when I walked in the classroom—this was October 1980—they said, "Are you going to leave us like the other teachers did?"

At Evander, Ms. Coram ran a very tight program. To this day I run into nurses and doctors who came out of my program. Then that program closed, and that's why I ended up at the School of Cooperative Technical Education in Manhattan. I went back to school again and got twenty-one credits in administration, and I've been there as an administrator since 1991.

I had a wonderful experience at Evander, which was the last of the academic high schools. It still had a music program with an orchestra, a band, and a choir. I was so naïve about music that at one of our ceremonies for the health careers, I asked a teacher if her students who did a cappella could sing, and she said, "certainly." These girls came down, and I said, "What are you going to sing?" They said, "My Love for You Will Never Die." I'm thinking it's one of those hip-hop songs or something, but it was a song that you hear on the radio. They were so professional.

I went back to Simpson Street a few times in the eighties. It used to look so huge. Now I see this tiny little area where I could stand on the corner and see Morris High School up the hill. It was a very emotional experience just to walk the streets. Of course, when new houses were built on Charlotte Street, the street President Jimmy Carter visited, it changed the face of the neighborhood a lot. You'd drive down the street that used to look huge and that you'd roller skate down, and you'd see this little narrow block. So yes, I've been back. They now call the Forty-First Precinct the Little House on the Prairie because there's so little around it.

Victoria Achibald-Good

Victoria Archibald–Good (1947–) is a social worker and a social work supervisor who has worked in this field in New York and Maryland.

My family moved to the Bronx from Harlem around 1950, and from what I remember, the move had a lot to do with housing. There wasn't a lot of affordable housing in those days. I'm not sure how long my parents were on the waiting list for public housing, but I do remember my mother saying that they were living in one room in my grandmother's place before we moved to the Patterson Houses. By the time we moved, I'd been born, my brother Tiny was born, and my mother was pregnant with a third child.

My earliest memory of the Bronx is going to P.S. 18, which was right around the corner from our apartment building. There were kids my age everywhere. We all went to the same school, and we didn't have to cross streets. But for some reason we always ended up at the candy store that was owned by Mr. Levi, and I always got to school late. I lived right around the corner from the school, and I was late. My teachers would ask my mother, "Well, what's going on in your household that she can't get out on time?" And my mother would reply, "Oh, she gets out on time." But my first stop was the candy store, for breakfast.

We had a lot of fun. Every summer we had a vacation day camp for the children in the projects. We went to museums on a regular basis, every single museum you could think of. We went to Coney Island, to baseball games, to the planetarium. There was a time during the summer that it didn't seem like we could relax because there was so much going on.

I started going to these places from the time I was in kindergarten, and then my sisters and brothers started going. Sometimes I got tired of going to the zoo every week because it seemed like I knew the Bronx Zoo like the back of my hand. We went to Prospect Park; we went to the Botanical Garden. I don't think there was one spot in the city that we didn't visit.

We moved to the Patterson Houses, which was on 144th Street, when I was three, and when I was growing up there, in the fifties and early sixties, it felt like a safe place. We could sit out on the benches all night until the sun came up and nobody would bother us. Everybody in the building knew who we were, and they'd look out for us. Everybody looked out for everybody.

Nobody had any real money, so the children would be taken to clinics. I remember going to the Guggenheim Dental Clinic in Manhattan, which I think probably traumatized many of us in the Bronx. It wasn't because the treatment was so bad. Most of the people who worked on our teeth were Indian dental students who treated us—how can I say this gently?—very roughly. They couldn't speak the language well, so they showed us what they wanted us to do by squeezing our neck or pinching our face or moving our head from one side to another. But it was free.

My mother used to go to the Lincoln Hospital clinic. When she had to go with my younger brothers and sisters, some other neighbor would babysit, and then my mother would reciprocate and babysit for that neighbor. That's what it was like. I remember the camaraderie and the supportiveness and the nurturing that I got from not only my own family but from folks in the building who weren't blood relatives.

The saying "It takes a village to raise a child": it was absolutely true in the Patterson Houses. But they also let you know when you were doing something wrong. They didn't hesitate to speak to you about dropping garbage in the hallway or talking too loud. All a neighbor had to do was say, "Don't let me tell your mother." That's all it took for us to rethink what we were doing because we knew we were going to have some problems if they told our mothers. And usually they didn't.

My best friend growing up, from elementary school through junior

high, was Theresa DePaulo. She lived in the building across the court-
yard from us. I haven't seen her in I don't know how long, but we were
close, and we loved each other dearly.

Her parents were elderly, and they died when we were in junior
high. The whole project came together to make sure she had food and
enough money to bury her parents. They took up a collection, and that
was typical of what went on in Patterson. When somebody died, it was
customary to bring a card with some money because people assumed
there was no insurance.

Patterson Houses was a very diverse place to grow up, and I remember
lots of Puerto Rican families. The Perez family lived right across the
hall from us on the fourth floor, and the Bonillas lived on the fourth
floor too. The Suarez family didn't live in the building, but I was good
friends with Geraldine Suarez.

I don't remember any friction or strife. There was the usual, kids
playing in the hallway or dropping garbage, but for the most part it was
a very tight-knit community, especially the building that I lived in.

I remember Mr. Bonilla used to make doughnuts for everybody. He
had this big pot of oil, and we would just sit on the stoop because we
could smell them from the stoop. And he would call us up when they
were ready, and everybody would get a freshly made doughnut. He also
had what they used to call Puerto Rican beer sitting on his window sill.
It looked like apple juice, and it was very foamy on the top. So he made
his beer, and he made the doughnuts to keep the kids happy and quiet.

When it came to teachers in elementary school and junior high, there
were only a few I would describe as being rough, and those were the
black teachers. They were very rigid. I probably appreciate it now more
than I did then because they were going to make sure that we got an
education. They weren't physically rough, and there was no corporal
punishment. But they didn't hesitate to call your parents if you weren't
doing your homework or working up to your potential.

I remember this one junior high school teacher, Mr. Blackman, who
said he wasn't only going to teach us earth science; he was also going to
teach us about life on the streets, about how it could harm us or even
destroy us. I remember him calling out to me from the window of the
school as we stood in front of the pizza shop nearby. "Victoria, aren't
you finished with that pizza yet?" he'd ask. "Yes, Mr. Blackman, I'm

coming," I'd call back. Because I knew that all he had to do was call my mother and I was in trouble.

It was in the sixth grade that I was first introduced to Latin music. Before then, I'd heard it because there were a lot of Latinos in our building, but I didn't really dance to it. As I got older, though, I began to notice more and more black people dancing to Latin music, and we just fell in love with it.

Have you ever heard the term Bootarican? Boot was a term that black people used to describe each other in the fifties and sixties. My friends and I think it was derived from the word bootblack, and it may have been a term of endearment.

When I first met my husband Harry, he would hear me and my friends talk about the Bootaricans in the Bronx, and he'd say, "What's a Bootarican?" And I said, "You can't have lived in New York and be black and not know what a Bootarican is." The term describes somebody who's both black and Puerto Rican. But he lived in a neighborhood where there were just black people and white people.

So we'd be somewhere, and we'd hear somebody speaking Spanish, somebody who looked just like us, and we'd say, "Uh, Bootarican." Harry and I recently went to a dance where Eddie Palmieri was playing. There was a woman singer from Puerto Rico there, and when she said, "All you Bootaricans out there," Harry turned to me and said, "You weren't lying." I said, "Why do you think I would lie? It may not be in the dictionary, but there is such a word." Anyway, Bootaricans describe some of the people I grew up with who either had a Puerto Rican mother and a black father or vice versa.

There was a lot of intermarrying. A lot of people say the Bronx was more multiracial and multiethnic at that time than a lot of other places in New York City and certainly in the country.

New York in the fifties had a lot of gangs. But they didn't call them gangs; they called them social clubs. And some of the guys I grew up with were always fighting somebody somewhere. There were a lot of projects in the Bronx, and there were all these rivalries. The young women could go to parties and dances whenever they wanted to, but the men had a harder time. I'd be sitting on a stoop or at my window, and all you'd see is guys from the projects running, and you knew someone was chasing them. They were either from the Forrest projects or the Melrose projects or the St. Mary's projects. They were always on the run. But they didn't use clubs and bats and guns. They fought with their fists.

People weren't getting killed, though. The guys in these clubs were very protective of the women in the projects. No matter where we were, we knew that someone was watching our back.

Another thing I remember from those years was the "booty train." I went to Walton High School, an all-girls' school, and it was one stop on the Woodlawn–Jerome line before the stop for DeWitt Clinton High School and Bronx Science. Guys who didn't even attend those schools used to get on the train and pull the emergency cord. The lights would go out, the train would stop, and they would feel women up.

I never had that problem. All I had to do was tell them I was from Patterson and that my father was insane, and they didn't bother me. But it was problematic for other young women on the train. I heard later that someone had gotten raped on the train.

It was my impression that when we moved to the Patterson Houses, most of the families were two-parent families. I think the Housing Authority had a law that you had to be married in order to live there. Initially, most of the families in our buildings had two parents present, and it stayed that way for a long time. I think mine was probably one of the few that was fractured. My father left when I was getting out of high school. But most of the families were intact, and in those that weren't, a parent had died. There was tremendous stability. Most of the families who were there when we arrived in the fifties were still there when we grew up and went to college.

It was a good place to grow up. For the most part, people were kind and generous and nurturing and supportive. It was a stable environment. I acquired a sense of stability not only in my own house but also from watching other families, the way they came together in a crisis.

Of course, by the late sixties all this had started to change. After I left, I started hearing really horrible stories about the siblings of some of the people I grew up with getting murdered in elevators. One of these was the Gorman family. There were twin girls, and they both got murdered in the same way—in an elevator by their boyfriends.

By the time I got to junior high school, my mother let me ride the train. A bunch of us had a club called the Socialettes, and we would go places on the subway. On Saturday mornings we'd skate at Central Park in winter and go to Coney Island in the summer. Coney Island was one of our favorite places because there always seemed to be cute guys there. There were also cute guys skating at Central Park at nine in the morning. I don't know where they came from, but we weren't real good skaters, and they kind of had to help us.

On the train, we could travel safely to just about any place in the city. By the time we were in ninth grade we were starting to go to dances in Manhattan. But there were still quite a few nice clubs in the Bronx. The Embassy Ballroom on 161st Street, which was in walking distance of where I lived, was one of my favorites. At the Embassy, you had live Latin music. You'd see Tito Puente and Celia Cruz and the Orchestra Broadway and Orchestra Harlow. It was a lot of fun, and really cheap. And Savoy Manor, on 149th Street, was within walking distance of the Patterson Houses. Sometimes they had live music, but most of the time it was a disco.

The main shopping strip in the South Bronx, 149th Street, was right near us and had a lot of shops, movies, dance halls, restaurants, and sandwich shops. There was this Italian sandwich shop, Joey's, that we'd save up to go to. They had these Italian sandwiches that would knock your eyes out. I think he's still there, on the corner of 149th Street and Morris Avenue.

Many years later, when I moved to Hempstead, on Long Island, and asked the guy at the deli for an Italian sandwich, he said, "I'm going to have to charge you a dollar for each different meat." When I protested, he said, "Where do you come from? You come from the Bronx, don't you?" And I said, "Yes, I do!" And he said, "Here we charge for every single item that we add." When I told him what kind of sandwiches I got in the Bronx, he said, "Yeah, we don't do that here."

We had dances big time in the Patterson Houses. The Socialettes had thirty-five-cent dances, and we bought clothes with the money we made from them. There were twelve of us, and each one of us had to have a dance every couple of weeks, depending on how much money we needed to buy clothes. It was a round-robin sort of thing. But we would have them in our apartments, and the parents were always there.

People came from all over the Bronx for these dances. And sometimes a fight would break out because some guy who was dating somebody in the Socialettes came from Forrest or St. Mary's, and he had to be very brave because he knew some stuff was going to get started at these dances. But we very rarely had to call the cops because somebody's father was always around to say, "All right. You can leave quietly, or we can escort you out." And before you knew it, quite a few fathers would be standing at the door.

During the Vietnam War, a lot of the guys I grew up with worried about being drafted. Many of them were talking about going to Canada. I guess these were the more militant brothers. They didn't believe that they could fight for a country that still discriminated against them. I don't think any of them went to Canada, and quite a few were eventually drafted.

I don't personally know anyone who died there, but many of the guys who came back didn't ever seem to be the same. They were the ones who got hooked on heroin. Many of us believed that they were already hooked before they got back home.

My friends and I were aware of the civil rights movement in the South, and I think it scared a lot of us because we were so young, and it was traumatic to watch people get hit by hoses and arrested and even die. But we hadn't been told of the personal experiences of a lot of the folks in the building, many of whom came from the South.

Our parents sheltered us. And although my parents were very in tune with what was going on in the South, theirs was not a Southern orientation. It was actually my paternal grandmother who kept memories of the South alive in our family. She had left the South, but it didn't seem like the South left her.

We used to go to her house, and she'd lay out cake and cookies, and I remember her saying one day, "You know, I didn't make that cake. Ii's a sto-bot cake."

And I said, "Gee, I wonder what kind of cake that is, sto-bot—that's a new one for me. How is it made?"

"You've never had sto-bot cakes before? It's a cake you buy from the sto."

But we didn't grow up eating Southern food. My father had an ulcer, so my mother didn't cook a lot of spicy foods or fatty foods, and as a result I felt somewhat deprived in the food department. I'd smell the chicken frying or chitlins being cooked in the hallway of our building, and I'd sit by somebody's door until they opened it, especially my next-door neighbor, Miss Eileen. She fried everything. And sometimes she'd knock on our door and say, "I just fried some chicken. You want some?" I'd look at my mother and she'd say, "Go ahead." Anything that was spicy or fatty we had to get from somebody else.

I had an opportunity to go to college at Tennessee State, but nobody thought I would be able to survive going to school in the South. My cousins, aunts, and uncles all said, "Now coming from the Bronx, living in New York, there's not a whole lot that you're going to take from anybody in the South. And we're concerned about you being there."

I wasn't the most militant person in the world, but we weren't used to our movements being restricted. We could go to any movie we wanted; we could shop on Thirty-Fourth Street or in Greenwich Village. I don't remember being humiliated by storekeepers or people working in movie theaters. I think it was because it was New York, and they weren't surprised to see black men and women shopping at places like Lord and Taylor's and Macy's. And so they treated us respectfully.

I remember heroin coming to the Bronx in the early sixties. Rita Johnson's brother, Vernon, was the first person I remember who got hooked. I remember my mother came upstairs and she said, "Vicki, you need to talk to Rita about getting her brother some help because he's wasted." The term she used was "strung out."

I remember seeing Vernon standing outside the building. This was a smart guy, bright as hell, and all of a sudden he was strung out. And because he lived next door, this was something that definitely got my attention. His sister did everything she could to encourage him to get treatment, to get counseling. Then I started hearing more stories about brothers and sisters and other folks in the projects getting hooked on drugs. So from what I could see, there was a major epidemic happening.

This was in the mid-sixties, when I was still in high school. And I definitely saw heroin as a major factor in dissolving the sense of community I grew up with. That and alcohol. I started to notice that they were both taking a huge toll on families.

It was mostly young men who were affected, and you knew who was doing heroin because they looked grimy. Some people were able to do heroin and still look clean, but at a certain point there was a new breed of heroin addict I wasn't used to seeing. All of a sudden you could tell who was strung out because they were dirty. They were unkempt, and their shoes were ragged.

This made me feel like I was living in a different world. It was so completely different from what I was used to that I felt I was living in a dream. And I wasn't the only one who felt that way. All of a sudden everyone in the projects was talking about break-ins, which were really difficult to do because the project doors were metal. People were saying these were inside jobs, that somebody was letting these folks in to burglarize people's apartments. Then I started hearing about folks who I grew up with getting thrown off rooftops because they were dealing. For the first time I started to feel fear, not only for myself but for the whole community.

I remember once, when I was still in high school, walking across the Willis Avenue Bridge to the Lincoln projects with my friend Rita. We used to do this all the time because we used to have to cross that bridge to shop on 125th Street. And here's this guy around our age, banging on top of this car, probably frustrated because he didn't have the money to get his fix. We just stood there and watched him. He was pummeling this car, he was kicking it, he was crying, he was sweating. And I remember feeling very sad about where the black community might be going because of heroin.

I hadn't known any white addicts. I didn't see any where I lived. But here I was in this huge housing complex, and there was a story every day about somebody who OD'd or who was thrown off a roof. Because not only were they addicted; they were trying to sell drugs and use the money to buy their own drugs.

This was the time when people said, "We've got to get out of here," although some people took more time to move out than others. I left in the late sixties, but my mother didn't move out until 1973 or 1974. And that was only because she was mugged on the way home from work. She got pretty bruised and battered, and that's when she said, "okay, I'm ready to go." I don't think she wanted to leave the Bronx, but she was able to move to Long Island because my brother Tiny was playing in the NBA at that time and had the money to get her a place.

Before my mother moved to Long Island, I had moved to the West Bronx and then to Yonkers. Starting in the early and mid-sixties, there was a migration of people who had saved enough money to move out. These were the people who could be described as approaching middle-class status because they were owners of barbershops, they were nurses. As soon as they had the money to leave, they did.

There was also a changed climate in the projects during those years. You couldn't go anywhere late. I remember one incident in 1964 when I was a senior in high school. It was in the summer and even at midnight, in that part of the Bronx, there were a lot of people in the street and on the benches. I got to my apartment building, and there was this guy in the lobby who I didn't know. At first I didn't think anything of it, but when I went to get the elevator, I saw him standing by the mail-boxes watching me.

When the elevator came, I felt so unsafe I decided not to get in. Instead, I left the building and knocked on the window of my friend Patricia's apartment, which was on the first floor. When her brother Bubba came to the window, I said, "Tell Tiny that I'm downstairs and that I think somebody followed me into the building."

Tiny came down, and in no time there were four or five guys, and they just chased this guy because they knew he was up to no good. Ordinarily I would have gotten on the elevator with this guy even though I didn't know him, because I didn't grow up with a sense of fear. But I remember feeling very afraid to get in the elevator that night.

Taur Orange

Taur Orange (1955–) is the director of the office of educational opportunity programs at the Fashion Institute of Technology, in New York City.

My mother was an only child, and my father was the youngest of nine. Both my parents were New Yorkers, but both sets of grandparents were from the South. On my father's side my grandmother was from Georgia, and my grandfather was from South Carolina. On my mother's side the grandparents were from Virginia.

My parents met in Harlem when my mom was eleven and my father was thirteen. The running joke in the family was that my mother showed my father how to take a shower because he was from what was called the Valley and she was from Sugar Hill. She loved to tease him about how the folks from the Valley didn't quite have it together, but the people up on Sugar Hill were a bit more civilized.

My father was a boxer. I'm not sure if he boxed professionally, but during World War II he was part of the Special Services unit, which was the entertainment branch of the American military. One of the perks of having served during World War II is that when he was discharged he was eligible for an apartment in a Quonset hut, a type of temporary housing that was built for returning veterans.

All this predates my birth, but I used to hear about these places from my parents, who lived in what's now called the Clason Point section of the Bronx. That was where the Quonset huts were and where my two older brothers were born. The next stop for the family was the Bronx-dale Houses in Soundview, which opened in the early 1950s and was one of the first public housing developments. My mom, dad, and two brothers were one of the first families to move in there, in 1953.

In the early days, most of the people who moved to the Bronxdale Houses were military families. There were three sections, with seven to ten buildings per section, and the tallest buildings were just six or seven stories. To this day I will not live anywhere that does not have trees and grass because that's what I saw every day looking out the window.

And the grass was amazingly well kept. You were not only fined if you stepped on the grass, but the person who did that was assigned to help maintain the grounds. All of the guys used to play stickball, punch ball, you name it, and if the ball went onto the grassy area it was quite a scene to watch the guys negotiate to see who was brave enough to go step on the grass to retrieve it.

When I was growing up, my dad worked three jobs. He worked for the Police Athletic League, for a private construction firm, and eventually for the New York City Transit Authority, then retired after forty-three years. He was not unlike most of the men at that time. They were very traditional in the sense that they expected the women to stay home and raise the children.

When I was young, the ethnic mix of the Bronxdale Houses was incredibly multiracial and multiethnic. There were a significant number of Italians, Jews, African Americans, and Latinos. At that time the pre-dominant Latino population was Puerto Rican. There were also a few people from India and the Philippines. When holidays like the Fourth of July would roll around or even on a typical summer day or summer night, you'd see all the mothers lined up in the evening watching their kids play. It looked like something from the United Nations.

Until the age of about twelve, we were very self-contained when it came to amusing ourselves. We played amongst ourselves right there on the grounds and didn't dare think of venturing beyond that. When we turned twelve or thirteen, especially the girls, we started venturing to the Monroe Houses, which was right across Bruckner Boulevard, because we thought that's where the finest boys were. But we always made sure we were back home before our parents realized we had ventured out.

The Bronxdale Houses had a community center, but most of the activities there were designed for boys. You had the cadets and different kinds of organized sports for the young men. The girls organized their own activities, and we played a lot of stoop games. We also played what we called popsies, off the sides of the building.

My family didn't attend a church regularly when I was growing up, but we were encouraged to attend with my cousins who lived in the Monroe Houses. My father was the eldest in his family, and most of his siblings always lived near him. Wherever he moved, they followed. This was a very close family. There was only one sibling who lived outside of walking distance, and she was based in Harlem. This was an entire family who benefited from New York City public housing.

Today, in hip-hop terminology, the projects, the PJs, is the term for fear and crime, and that's probably as it should be. But we're talking about the late fifties up through the mid-1970s, and it was an environment that was almost entirely drug free. That was the norm. It's very different now where the norm is that public housing is an environment that's drug active.

I come from a family where music is sort of in the DNA. My father was a drummer. My oldest brother was a drummer. My second brother, who was a horn player, went to Music and Art High School. I played oboe and flute. Everyone in my extended family as well as my nuclear family either took music lessons or voice lessons.

Everybody was aware that my Uncle Joe, Joseph Orange, was a professional musician. My middle brother was an aspiring jazz musician, and he was always able to let us know who my uncle was playing with. My oldest brother, Richard Orange Jr., was very heavily into poetry and at one point was a member of the Last Poets, groups of poets and musicians who rose from the black nationalist movement of the late sixties. And J. C. Higginbotham, who was a famous jazz trombonist, was also a relative.

Music was played in our house all the time. We grew up listening to everything from *South Pacific* to *Soul Train* and everything in between.

There was a great deal of harmony where I grew up, but there were also pockets of bigotry that manifested themselves and surfaced among kids. Whenever the boys would fight, the first things that would come out of their mouths were racial epithets. And this was on both sides. It was not uncommon for African American kids to be called nigger and for white kids to be called honkies.

And here's the strange thing. Somehow the Italian kids escaped a lot of the racial confrontations because they were seen as people of color even though they didn't want to own up to it. They were deluding themselves in thinking that they were white. They had an African ancestry that they denied.

In my house, politics wasn't discussed in terms of it being politics. It was discussed in terms of life skills, and much of that came from my mother. Back in the late fifties and early sixties, when White Castle would not serve people of color, my mother took part in the picketing against them. She went to the branch near Bronxdale, not the one on Allerton Avenue and Boston Road, where there was so much violence.

She and my father talked about her doing this. There was a lot of concern about her being involved because there was a fear of violence. This was in 1963, so I must have been about eight, and my brothers and I weren't allowed to see her picket. But I remember the intensity with which my father tried to convince my mother not to picket, how he told her that there could be repercussions.

There was a lot of discussion in my home about what was going on during the sixties, about ways to address bigotry, and what we were to do if someone called us a name.

I especially remember an episode involving my middle brother. When he was in fifth grade, he was selected by the teacher to be part of a class play, which was *Huckleberry Finn*. I don't need to tell you who he was asked to play. My mother just about lost her mind when she learned that her son Tony was asked to play Jim the slave. Tony was ten, maybe eleven. This would have been maybe 1960, and the episode still stays with me. For days it was the only subject discussed in my home.

My father wanted to take a slightly less aggressive stance. He suggested sending a letter. My mother said hell no. It wasn't a matter of if she was going to go over to the school but when. She was going to have a discussion with the teacher who asked my brother to play a slave.

I can't say that teachers routinely put me or other African American youngsters in humiliating or difficult positions. But I remember one thing. I was, as I am now, a compulsive gum chewer. When I was in the sixth grade, I had a teacher who would insist that I swallow the gum I was chewing. That used to be the practice back in those days. If you were caught chewing gum in class, you had to swallow it. But I was aware that she never asked any of the young white women to swallow their gum. She'd chastise them, she might threaten to contact their parents, but she'd never make them swallow it. She'd let them spit it out. With me it was always swallow it. There was a double standard.

When it came to education, my parents were like the majority of parents. The expectation was that if the father and/or mother were out busting their butts to put food on the table, we were expected to hold down our job, and our job was to put 120 percent into every single day. Not some days, every day. It was the norm for parents, at least the mothers, to check homework every single night so as to monitor our progress, not because the schools requested or required it but because our parents had an investment in monitoring us.

And this went on not just in our house but also in our friends' houses. There was a time when we knew not to be on the telephone because that was when our parents were checking homework.

Some of those friendships crossed racial lines, but more for my brothers and less for the girls. The interracial friendships for the girls took place primarily in the schools. Once we came home, we tended to be with the same ethnic group. The boys, however, always crossed racial and ethnic lines, in part, I think, because of a common interest in sports.

When girls started dating—for me, this was in the late sixties and early seventies—those same lines tended to be preserved. African American girls stayed with African American boys. Occasionally they dated a Latino boy. The Filipinos went both ways. They dated Latinos, African Americans, and occasionally whites.

My mother was an absolute genius. Every holiday she'd conduct what she called a trip to nowhere. She'd let me and my brothers rotate holidays. Easter it might be my choice, Thanksgiving it might be one of my brothers' choice. We'd get to select a train line. She'd pack a lunch for us, and we'd ride to the end of that line just to see what was there. We'd explore the community, have lunch, and then take the train back home. This allowed us to develop a comfort with traveling anywhere in the city and familiarized us with all of the train lines. It also opened our eyes to the communities beyond where we lived. There was the excitement and anticipation of figuring out what was at the end of that train ride.

My mother also took us to museums, but these trips supplemented the museum visits. We just went to different communities and hung out. And it was affordable, which was good because my parents didn't have a lot of money.

My family and I also attended live music events anywhere and everywhere that was affordable. We saw James Brown, the Jackson Five, the Temptations at the Apollo.

In terms of our musical training, it took place in schools, and we also got private lessons. There used to be a music school on Westchester Avenue near Elder Avenue, and that's where my brothers and I took our music lessons. When we attended high school, we had a choice between typing or music lessons. My mother insisted upon music lessons, and to this day I still type with three fingers.

My mother began to work part time when I was five, and when I turned six and went into the first grade, she began to work full time as a paraprofessional. In those days, a lot of mothers who were entering the workforce were encouraged to be part of the educational system because that way they could be close to their children. There was also the feeling that mothers had a lot to offer in terms of childrearing and education. So many mothers were encouraged to become paraprofessionals, where they'd assist a teacher in the classroom.

My mother was a paraprofessional for many years before her lead teacher urged her to return to college and complete her education. She had dropped out of college when it was time to raise her children, but she went back to school and went on to become a classroom teacher and teach high school English.

Students were tracked when I was in school with SP classes—I forgot what that even stands for—and I began to see a pattern of encouragement for some kids and not so much support for other kids. For my parents, the big issue was whether their children were going to get a certain kind of social experience that paralleled the educational experience. The fear with the SP classes was that even though they offered an accelerated educational experience, my parents wanted me and my brothers to have a parallel social experience. I got into SP, but my mother made the decision to keep me in the three-year SP, not the one where you'd skip a year.

Our teachers were very involved with us, to the point of knowing probably more about our family lives than I think teachers now do, except for the exceptional teachers. And there was cooperation between parents and teachers all the time, so much so that we tried to strategize on how to get around that. Teachers thought nothing of calling homes. Parents thought nothing of calling teachers or even dropping in to school during the day. And of course parents, as I mentioned earlier, were always required and expected to sign off on homework. It was unacceptable for a student to bring homework in the next day without a parent signature.

When I was growing up, much of what I learned about the civil rights movement and the Black Panthers I learned at home. That sort of thing was almost never discussed in the schools. I don't remember Martin Luther King being discussed until I was in junior high. And to my recollection African American history and African American culture weren't part of what was going on in school at all. My consciousness and awareness of these issues came from my home. I don't remember if there was a point at which I started to think of myself as a political person. Primarily this was because I was raised in a home where you were not just an individual; you were an individual who represented a race. That was articulated early on.

Also, our neighborhood was a bit removed geographically from the terrible abandonment and disinvestment and arson that occurred in the South Bronx. We were not in that area. But during the seventies I used to experience that sort of thing on a daily basis—the fires, the burning down of the South Bronx—because it was my bus routes and my train route, the no. 6 line, the Pelham line, to and from high school. Every month there was another fire.

And Bronx Science, where I went to high school, was tough. There was a black student organization called BOSS, the Black Organization for Student Strength. The Latino students were with us, but eventually they developed a separate organization. The lines between African Americans and Latinos were very thin. Socially and culturally, we were aligned with each other.

Bronx Science was clearly a rigorous academic environment that I was not emotionally or psychologically ready for, having come from J.H.S. 125. It's one thing to be a big fish in a little sea and another to be a smaller fish in a larger sea.

But it was during my high school years that I came into my own politically. The consciousness and the awareness were always present, but the involvement, the activity came during these years. There was a citywide organization that was spearheaded by Kwame Ture, who was then known as Stokely Carmichael and who had been a student at Science. He was years ahead of me, but he always came back to Science to recruit. I fell in with a group of students from various high schools from throughout the city, and that's how I began to find my political aware-ness and begin my political activity.

This organization was more national than local, and it also had an international focus. Even then Brother Kwame had a vision of a pan-African forum for students. We were all encouraged to connect with other students from throughout the city, the state, the country, and even the Caribbean. I recall meeting students from a lot of different campuses around the country. I can't remember some of the highlights of that experience, but there are a thousand of them, I'm sure.

I had an Afro in those days. But I think that was as much a part of the youth culture as part of the black power culture. Everybody wore headbands and bellbottoms and had an Afro pick, and I went right along with them.

Walking Tour of Morrisania

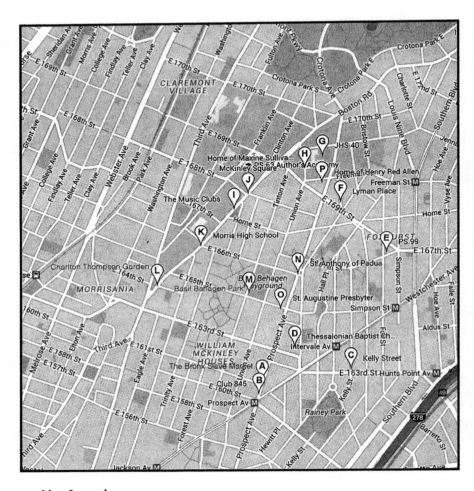

Map Legend

A The Bronx Slave Market
B Club 845
C Kelly Street
D Thessalonian Baptist Church
E P.S. 99
H Home of Maxine Sullivan
I The Music Clubs

J McKinley Square
K Morris High School
L Charlton Thompson Garden
O St. Augustine Presbyterian Church
   and Fellowship House
P Home of Henry Red Allen

Walking Tour of Morrisania

In the mid-1930s, a small number of African American families, many of them headed by Pullman porters or postal workers, began to rent apartments in a predominantly Jewish working-class community along Prospect Avenue, in a section of the South Bronx where the Depression had created housing vacancies. Seeking larger apartments and better educational opportunities for their children than they could find in Harlem, these pioneering black families moved into a community with tree-lined streets, good schools, excellent shopping and public transportation, and a socialist and trade union tradition that muted some of the hostility blacks normally met when they settled in white neighborhoods.

As more and more families in Harlem heard that spacious apartments were available in a safe, multiracial neighborhood, this trickle swelled to a flood, making Morrisania the largest community of people of African descent in the Bronx. Afro-Caribbeans and Puerto Ricans soon joined the migration, creating a substantial black and Latino presence in Hunts Point, a multiethnic community southeast of Morrisania.

By the mid-1940s, a unique community had begun to emerge in this corner of the southeastern Bronx. By the early 1960s "white flight" had transformed Morrisania into a completely black and Latino neighborhood, and racism remained a stubborn and corrosive force in the lives of its black residents. Yet for a twenty-year period, roughly from 1935 to 1955, blacks, whites, and Latinos lived, worked, and went to school together in Morrisania far more harmoniously than they did in most sections of the city. The result was a cross-fertilization of cultures that bred an extraordinary musical tradition and helped many youngsters who grew up in this community become leaders in education, the arts, politics, business, and the professions.

A tour of historic black Morrisania, following a route charted by the Bronx African American History Project, helps tell the story of this remarkable community. Highlights of the tour include the important institutions of Morrisania from the 1930s through the late 1970s, notably its churches and schools, its theaters and nightclubs, and the places where people congregated for shopping, recreation, political action, or musical and artistic creativity. Also included are places where cultural innovation took place in later periods, particularly the rise of hip-hop and the creation of the Old Timers' Day reunions that for more than forty years have celebrated this community's history on the first Sunday in August.

"The Bronx Slave Market," 161st Street and Prospect Avenue

During the Depression, African American women lined up on selected street corners in the Bronx, one of which was at 161st Street and Prospect Avenue, to get day work cleaning the houses of white families. White housewives would walk through the crowd and try to bargain with the women to do their housework for the lowest possible price. The NAACP, black church groups, and local labor unions worked hard to end this demoralizing ritual and gain recognition for domestics by unions and employment agencies. The Rev. Edler Hawkins of St. Augustine's Presbyterian Church, on 165th Street and Prospect Avenue, was Morrisania's most impassioned and effective opponent of the slave market, and the institution had largely disappeared by the end of World War II.

Club 845, 845 Prospect Avenue

This was the site of Club 845, which from the 1930s through the 1960s was a major center of cultural life in Morrisania. Some of the era's best-known jazz artists, such as Dizzy Gillespie, Thelonious Monk, and Tony Bennett, performed at the club in its heyday, and church and community groups rented the club for dances and fundraising events. The club closed in the late 1960s when Morrisania began losing housing and population, but the address retained its importance in American music history. The Burger King that opened on that site in the 1970s reinvented itself as the

Burger King Disco during the hip-hop era, providing a platform for local hip-hop legends such as Love Bug Starski.

Kelly Street and Environs

The block of Kelly Street between East 163rd Street and Westchester Avenue was the block where U.S. Secretary of State Colin Powell and former New York City Landmarks Commissioner Gene Norman grew up. Hunts Point, to which many Afro-Caribbeans moved from Harlem in the 1940s, was a multiethnic working-class neighborhood, and this block had a vibrant street life that brought together children of African, Jewish, Italian, Greek, and Puerto Rican ancestry.

Neighborhood landmarks included the Tropicana Club, a popular Latin music venue during the 1950s and 1960s, around the corner on Westchester Avenue. J.H.S. 5 and St. Margaret's Episcopal Church, where many Afro-Caribbean families worshipped, were located farther south on Kelly Street. Nearby, on Tiffany Street, is St. Athanasius Roman Catholic Church, a small parish church that became a leader in sponsoring affordable new and rehabilitated housing for the community from the 1960s to the present.

Hunts Point Palace, 163rd Street and Southern Boulevard

This was the most important music venue in the South Bronx from World War I to the early 1970s and a symbol of the blending of musical cultures in Morrisania and Hunts Point. All of the great Latin, calypso, rhythm and blues, and jazz groups played the "Palace" in the 1940s, 1950s, and 1960s, and its "breakfast dances," which began at 10 p.m. and ended at dawn, are still remembered fondly by old timers. Among the performers who played the Hunts Point Palace in its heyday were Charlie Parker, Dizzy Gillespie, Dexter Gordon, James Brown, Jackie Wilson, Sonny Till and the Orioles, the Mighty Sparrow, Tito Rodriguez, and Tito Puente.

Thessalonia Baptist Church, 163rd Street and Stebbins Avenue (also known as Rev. James Polite Avenue)

Thessalonia Baptist Church, which started in the 1930s as a small congregation on Eagle Avenue, was headed by a dynamic pastor named James Polite and grew in tandem with black Morrisania, evolving into one of

New York City's largest Baptist churches. Located on the former site of a Jewish synagogue, Thessalonia has been a powerful force for development in Morrisania, housing on its premises a public school and investing heavily in the construction of new housing on the blocks adjoining the church.

Public School 99, Stebbins Avenue and Home Street

P.S. 99, a large public elementary school, was one of the major centers of cultural life in Morrisania in the 1950s. Its afternoon and night center, headed by the legendary Vincent Tibbs, sponsored sports programs and organized talent shows where some of Morrisania's most famous doo-wop singers performed. Twenty years later, P.S. 99 remained in the forefront of music history as the site of some of the hip-hop star Grandmaster Flash's outdoor jams.

Lyman Place

This one-block street between 169th Street and Freeman Street, which was settled by African American and Afro-Caribbean families in the 1940s, was home to an unusually large number of residents who achieved distinction in the arts. The great bebop pianist Elmo Hope lived on Lyman Place, and one of his regular visitors was Thelonious Monk, who lived on the block for three years in the 1960s after his Upper West Side apartment caught fire. The jazz drummer Leo Mitchell, the actor Robinson Frank Adu, and the journalist and author Elise Washington also grew up on the block. In the 1970s Lyman Place was saved from the wave of arson and abandonment that hit surrounding blocks by Hetty Fox, who moved back from California to start the New York Kids Foundation, an organization that has served local children for more than thirty years.

Junior High School 40, Prospect Avenue Between Ritter Place and Jennings Street

J.H.S. 40, a public junior high school in Morrisania, had one of the best music programs in the city in the 1940s and 1950s, sponsoring two concert bands, an orchestra, and a jazz band. Any student in the music program could take home an instrument to practice, and a number of talented musicians, as well as successful professionals in other fields, were products of this school.

Maxine Sullivan Residence, Ritter Place west of Prospect Avenue

This was the home of the jazz singer Maxine Sullivan, a big-band singing star of the late 1930s and 1940s who sponsored jazz performances at her home for friends and neighbors in Morrisania and who founded a youth center on Stebbins Avenue called "The House That Jazz Built."

The Music Clubs of Boston Road

In the 1950s and 1960s, Boston Road between 167th Street and 169th Street was home to three major music clubs: Goodson's, Freddy's, and Sylvia's Blue Morocco. People from throughout the Bronx and the city came to hear artists like Nancy Wilson, the Jimmy Castor Bunch, and Mickey and Sylvia. Thanks to these clubs, Morrisania residents were able to hear great live music at locations within walking distance of their homes.

McKinley Square

McKinley Square, the area bounded by Boston Road, Franklin Avenue, and 168th and 169th Streets, was the center of political, cultural, commercial, and intellectual life in historic Morrisania, home to the Morrisania Library, the Lincoln Republic Club, and the Jackson Democratic Club, as well as to many stores and restaurants. In the 1950s and 1960s, McKinley Square was filled with strollers and shoppers during the day and with sharply dressed clubgoers on Friday and Saturday nights. During the hip-hop era, P.S. 63, the elementary school on McKinley Square, was a major venue for outdoor hip-hop jams.

Morris High School, 166th Street and Boston Road

This beautiful landmarked building houses Morris High School, which celebrated its hundredth anniversary in 2004. In the 1940s and 1950s, Morris High School was the most racially integrated high school in New York City and possibly the United States, offering an outstanding academic program and first-rate instruction in the arts. Its graduates from the Morrisania area, among them public servants including Colin Powell and musicians including Valerie Simpson, have achieved distinction in many walks of life. Although the school deteriorated in the 1970s and 1980s, in recent years it has experienced something of a renaissance and boasts a national championship robotics team.

Charlton Garden, 164th Street and Boston Road

Charlton Garden is a community park named in 1952 for Sergeant Cornelius H. Charlton, a Korean War Congressional Medal of Honor recipient. Leroy Archible and Bob Gumbs, researchers for the Bronx African American History Project, have formed an organization called the Friends of Charlton Garden to oversee the restoration of the park and rename it in honor of Private First Class William Thompson, also a Korean War Medal of Honor recipient from the Bronx, and other community veterans.

Basil Behagen Park, Tinton Avenue and 166th Street

This community park, which is sometimes called 23 Park because it was built on the former site of P.S. 23, has been the site of Old Timers' Day reunions for Morrisania residents since the late 1960s. Past and current residents of Morrisania come to barbecue, listen to music, and watch neighborhood basketball greats compete against one another. 23 Park also has hip-hop significance, as Grandmaster Flash used to hold schoolyard jams there in the 1970s. Current hip-hop star Fat Joe, who grew up in the Forest Houses across the street, sponsors a basketball tournament there.

St. Anthony of Padua Parish and School, 166th Street and Prospect Avenue

St Anthony's was a center of African American Catholic life in Morrisania from the 1940s through the 1960s. Its elementary school offered a first-rate education from first through eighth grades and had an excellent choir and sports teams. Among the most famous graduates of St. Anthony's parish school were the Chantels, whose 1957 hit "Maybe" was the first song by a female vocal group to sell a million records.

St. Augustine's Presbyterian Church and Fellowship House, 165th Street and Prospect Avenue

St. Augustine's has been a major center of spiritual, political, and intellectual life in Morrisania since the late 1930s, when a brilliant young minister, the Rev. Edler Hawkins, was dispatched to Morrisania to build a congregation among local African American families. A theologian, civil rights leader, and mentor to the neighborhood's youth, Rev. Hawkins transformed St. Augustine's into a place where the nation's leading civil rights leaders, including Dr. Martin Luther King Jr., came to speak and where the best and brightest of Morrisania's young people found guidance and inspiration. When the Rev. Hawkins left St. Augustine's in the 1960s to become the first African American professor at Princeton's divinity school, he had persuaded many local young people to follow him into the ministry.

Conclusion

The stories in this book raise a number of important issues for scholars of urban African American history as well as for teachers, students, and policy makers seeking to understand the history of the Bronx.

First, these stories defy images of the Bronx as a place that nurtured Jewish, Italian, and Irish dreams of a middle-class lifestyle until blacks and Latinos moved in. Contrary to popular belief, the Bronx was a place that also nurtured comparable dreams for tens of thousands of blacks and Latinos in the 1940s, 1950s, and early 1960s. Even though huge "Old Timers'" reunions at Crotona Park and Bronx housing projects suggest that many blacks and Latinos over the age of sixty-five have overwhelmingly positive memories of growing up in the Bronx, that idea has not yet penetrated the popular consciousness. These oral histories will help correct this misconception and force us to take a new look at black migration and community development in the borough.

Second, these stories describe the peaceful integration of a neighborhood, an event that was extraordinarily rare not only in New York but around the nation. It is hard to think of another community where landlords could have put up signs in the early 1930s reading "We rent to select Colored tenants" without provoking massive resistance, another community where the arrival of black families took place without significant episodes of harassment or violence. The uniqueness of this experience is underlined, in the oral histories, by stories of the harassment our subjects experienced when they left Morrisania to go to other parts of the Bronx, such as the Grand Concourse or Fordham Road. This raises the question:

What made the racial atmosphere in Morrisania different from that of so many other urban neighborhoods?

Third, the stories describe how public institutions commonly thought of as failing blacks and Latinos, especially public schools and public housing, provided a setting within which family aspirations were reinforced, at least for some residents. And so we must ask: What features of Bronx schools and housing projects in the 1940s and 1950s made them places that black and Latino families viewed in largely positive terms? And why did that positive experience not continue?

Finally, given all these positive community experiences, why were the neighborhoods where they took place so hard hit by disinvestment, arson, crime, and drugs from the late 1960s through the late 1970s? Why did Morrisania and neighboring Hunts Point experience so much depopulation, abandonment, and arson—so much devastation that people came from around the world to see the damage? How could these communities have been "successful" if they collapsed so precipitously when economic and political conditions changed?

Let me start by discussing a key issue, the obliteration of historical memory.

The obliteration of historical memory in black communities is not confined to the Bronx. A landmark work in urban African American history, set in Chicago, is a two-volume set of oral histories called *Bridges of Memory*, compiled by Timuel Black. Like *Before the Fires*, much of it focuses on the period before the civil rights movement, when Chicago's black neighborhoods were home to thriving business districts, clubs and theaters that were centers of musical creativity, and residents filled with energy, optimism, and hope. Black Chicago neighborhoods, though far more racially homogeneous than Morrisania, had many of the same features—strong churches, great class diversity, and public schools—that served the needs of residents surprisingly well despite the racism prevailing in most of the city.

A recent book about Detroit, David Maraniss's *Once in a Great City: A Detroit Story*, presents a similar picture, focusing on the great music traditions in black Detroit during the 1950s and early 1960s as well as the rise of Motown. Similar narratives could easily be developed regarding black communities in Newark, Philadelphia, Washington, and a score of other American cities. Although historians have been slow to recognize it, the period from the early 1940s to the early 1960s, before the passage of the great civil rights acts and before corporate America and the nation's top universities had any significant black presence, may turn out to be the time of the greatest economic progress in urban black communities.

What happened in subsequent years—the urban uprisings of the 1960s, the deindustrialization and disinvestment of the 1970s and 1980s, the crack epidemic of the late 1980s and early 1990s—left these communities a shadow of their former selves. But the vitality they displayed during the war and postwar years needs to be given greater attention and analyzed in greater depth.[1]

What makes the Bronx portion of this story unusual is not the vitality of the communities that emerged there, which reflects a national pattern, but the racial and cultural diversity of the neighborhoods in which blacks lived during the 1930s and 1940s. Given the violence that greeted blacks who moved into formerly white neighborhoods in Detroit, as documented by Thomas J. Sugrue in *Origins of the Urban Crisis: Race and Inequality in Postwar Detroit*, or that greeted blacks who moved into lower Washington Heights, as documented by Robert W. Snyder in *Crossing Broadway: Washington Heights and the Promise of New York City*, why were blacks able to move into previously all-white Morrisania without violence and without apparent opposition of any kind?[2]

The answer to this question may lie in traditions of trade unionism and political radicalism, heavily influenced by the Communist Party, that shaped the attitudes of residents of Morrisania and the adjoining communities of Hunts Point and Crotona Park East. During the first four years of the Depression, the northern portion of Morrisania was the site of a rent revolt of epic proportions, leading to pitched battles between residents, city marshals, and police, involving thousands of people.[3] When this protest died down, residents organized sit-ins at newly organized home relief offices to make sure that residents got the aid they needed to keep them in their apartments.[4]

Though few blacks were involved in these protests, Bronx rent strikers and relief protesters were exposed to the message of militant racial egalitarianism that the Communist Party espoused during the early Depression years and insisted its followers adhere to. Not only did anyone attending a communist-led rally in the early Depression see the slogan "Black and White Unite and Fight" displayed at demonstrations, but many were mobilized to attend marches through Harlem to "Free the Scottsboro boys" (nine young black defendants in Alabama facing death following a manufactured rape accusation). And all had heard of communists being expelled or put on trial for "white chauvinism" if they made racist statements.[5]

In the New York City of the early 1930s, if you were going to choose a neighborhood that upwardly mobile black families could move into peacefully, you could do no better than choose one that had a significant communist influence. Understanding this helps put the Morrisania/ Hunts Point story in perspective. Not everyone in those neighborhoods was a communist, a communist sympathizer, or an antiracist. But enough antiracist whites lived in those communities to undermine the hostility, violence, and exclusion that blacks faced in nearly every other part of the Bronx, not only Irish neighborhoods such as Mott Haven or Italian neighborhoods such as Belmont but also the middle-class Jewish neighborhoods on and near the Grand Concourse.[6]

This not only meant that individual black families and black children were free from harassment or assault when they moved in but also that Morrisania's transition from being a white neighborhood to a black and Latino one took place over twenty years, not four or five, and that many black children in the community, right through the mid-1950s, attended integrated schools.

Morris High School, the neighborhood's signature public high school, was integrated right through the early 1950s, in large part because white parents and the school's principal, who described the institution as a "little United Nations," fought to keep it that way.[7] That voluntary integration was not the norm in much of the Bronx in the 1950s is reflected in the long and bitter campaigns to end white-only policies in the Bronx's largest private housing complex, Parkchester, and in the huge Castle Hill Beach Club, neither of which accepted blacks until the late 1950s. Even as late as 1963, mob violence greeted civil rights protesters at a White Castle on Allerton Avenue and Boston Road. The relative racial harmony in Morrisania and Hunts Point was, sadly, more the exception than the rule in the Bronx—and in the rest of New York City—from the 1930s to the 1960s.[8]

The one place where such integration did occur, though it was not entirely voluntary and did not last long, was in the Bronx's public housing projects, most of which opened in the early 1950s. Victoria Archibald-Good and Taur Orange, who grew up in the Patterson and Bronxwood Houses, respectively, describe residents effortlessly crossing racial and cultural barriers in child care and friendship networks and benefitting from excellent building maintenance and strong public services. While neither the integration nor the high quality of maintenance lasted through the 1960s, these benefits gave those who experienced them as children extremely positive memories of life in public housing.[9]

This raises an important question with implications for public policy. Every person interviewed in this book attended integrated schools and/or lived in multiracial neighborhoods or public housing projects. Did this contribute to the success so many of them achieved later in life?

To address this question, I'd like to share some reflections by Dr. Vincent Harding, the civil rights leader, that offer clues to why some black students from low- or moderate-income families were able to thrive in Bronx public schools. Dr. Harding spoke of two early influences that shaped his development as a scholar and civil rights leader—the encouragement in preaching and public speaking he received at the small all-black West Indian church he attended and the mentoring and guidance he received from mostly white teachers at Morris High School. As a result of his church experience, Harding concluded, he came to Morris with great self-confidence; this gave him a foundation upon which teachers in the school could build. And at Morris, from which he eventually graduated as valedictorian, he encountered teachers who pushed him to develop his writing abilities, encouraged him to pursue higher education, and gave him jobs that helped finance his college education.

Harding was not the only person interviewed who had the benefit of exposure to strong black institutions while attending integrated schools. Almost all of the people represented in this book attended black churches, and a few attended all-black summer camps associated with those churches. Institutions such as St. Augustine's Presbyterian Church in Morrisania, whose brilliant minister, the Rev. Edler Hawkins, exposed his young parishioners to some of the greatest black musicians and political leaders of the era and gave them an opportunity to showcase their own skills, were an integral part of what made Bronx African American communities of the 1940s and 1950s places where many young people from families of modest means were inspired to imagine themselves as successful professionals.[10]

But the multiracial public schools they attended also had programs and resources, some of which no longer exist, that played an important role in nurturing students in low- and moderate-income communities. In the 1940s, 1950s, and 1960s, New York City public schools, which were among the best funded in the nation, had extraordinary music, sports, and afterschool programs, and these provided valuable training and mentoring for young people along with much-needed safe zones from gang violence or troubled families. Until the fiscal crisis of the mid-1970s led to draconian budget cuts, many middle schools in the Bronx had hundreds of musical instruments that any student who tried out for and made the band or the orchestra could take home to practice with. Equally import-ant, every elementary school was open from 3 to 5 and 7 to 9 p.m. for supervised activities, which included everything from arts and crafts to talent shows to organized basketball.[11]

These programs did not guarantee success for every student. The Bronx public schools were heavily tracked: students were organized in classes according to their perceived ability, determined by testing. Many had teachers who were mediocre and did not always deal respectfully with black students, especially those students whose parents did not visit the school regularly. But more than a few black students in these schools thrived, and their talents and skills were identified and nurtured. Some of that nurturing and mentoring occurred in classrooms, but much of it occurred in bands, orchestras, choruses, school publications, athletic pro-grams, and afterschool centers.[12]

Bronx public schools, for all their limitations, were true community centers, places that were open from early morning until the evening and that offered outlets for a wide variety of abilities. The talented people whose stories are told here were among the beneficiaries. One hopes that young people growing up in the same neighborhoods today have comparable opportunities.

This brings us to another important question. Why, if these commu-nities provided such opportunities for young people in the 1940s, 1950s, and early 1960s, did they deteriorate so rapidly over the next twenty years? Why did Morrisania lose 50 percent of its population between 1970 and 1980 and see much of its housing stock abandoned and destroyed by fires? How could such a terrible thing have taken place in a community with strong churches, good schools, and residents who, for the most part, saw their neighborhood as a positive place?

Here is my theory. What happened to the South Bronx is not attrib-utable to any inherent weakness in its neighborhoods or people, or to de-stabilizing events such as the construction of the Cross Bronx Expressway, but to national and global shifts in capital and investment that eventually wreaked similar devastation on many urban areas. There have been mul-tiple explanations for the wave of arson and disinvestment that swept through the Bronx in the late 1960s and 1970s, ranging from the loss of manufacturing jobs (more than five hundred thousand from 1945 to 1976), to the rising prices of heating oil, to the closing of Bronx firehouses, to a rapid outmigration of the South Bronx's black and Latino middle class as a result of the Mitchell Lama program.[13] All these explanations have some merit. But in my opinion, the first one is most important, especially when comparing what happened to the Bronx to what happened elsewhere in the nation. In the late 1970s, people came from all over the world to view the stretches of vacant lots in Crotona Park East, at the north end of Morrisania, but by the early 1990s similar vistas could be seen in a score of northern and Midwestern cities where factory closures had occurred, from Bridgeport, Connecticut, to Buffalo, New York, to Camden, New Jersey, to Youngstown, Ohio, to Gary, Indiana, to East St. Louis, Illinois.

Today, the South Bronx is far less unusual in the degree of devastation that took place in its neighborhoods than it is in the degree to which its neighborhoods have been rebuilt. Starting with the area just east of Crotona Park, which was first developed with single-family homes, virtually every vacant lot and burned-out area in Morrisania and Hunts Point has been filled with townhouses, apartment buildings, and shopping centers fought for and built by local nonprofit organizations with the help of subsidies and tax credits offered at the local, state, and federal level. If you stand at the intersection of Boston Road and Charlotte Street, where President Jimmy Carter and foreign heads of state once came to view fifteen blocks of uninterrupted devastation, new construction is visible as far as the eye can see.

To anyone who lived though the fires as a resident or visited the community in horror after the damage had run its course, what has taken place in Morrisania and Hunts Point is inspiring beyond words. No neighborhood in the nation that experienced comparable devastation when its industrial economy imploded, certainly not Buffalo, Youngstown, Philadelphia, Baltimore, or Detroit, all of which I have spent time in, has been rebuilt to this degree. The South Bronx neighborhoods described in these oral histories, once derided for their precipitous collapse, have become an American urban success story.[14]

Now that the rebuilding of the South Bronx has entered public consciousness—to the point where real estate developers have targeted it as a new frontier for investment—it may be time for a new look at the African American communities that emerged in the Bronx during the 1930s, 1940s, and 1950s and at the legacy they provide for future residents. Some of the people whose stories appear in this book, among them Hetty Fox, Arthur Crier, Howie Evans, James Pruitt, Beatrice Bergland, and Gene Norman, played roles as activists, educators, and civil servants in helping the neighborhoods they grew up in survive, recover, and rebuild. The black churches they attended played an important role in uniting residents and helping them reclaim their communities and build new housing on once-vacant lots. Even the Bronx's much-maligned public schools and housing projects, which remained open during the worst years of the devastation and continued to serve neighborhood residents when private housing markets collapsed and business districts atrophied, must be credited with helping make survival and recovery possible.

The story of black settlement and community development in the Bronx, which is currently being revised and rewritten by new waves of African and West Indian immigrants, is one with many lessons to teach us about race, class, culture, and the changing shape of American cities. It is hoped that this book will help correct longstanding stereotypes, encourage discussion about what kinds of policies work best to encourage educational and economic progress among people of modest means, and contribute to the transformation of cities into places that serve all their residents well.

Biographies

Victoria Archibald-Good, a graduate of Fordham University, is the sister of Nate "Tiny" Archibald, one of the greatest basketball players ever to come out of New York City, who grew up with her in the Patterson Houses and attended the same public schools—P.S. 18 and Clark J.H.S. After graduating from Walton High School and from Fordham, she pursued a career as a social worker, rising to high positions in social work administration in Nassau County before moving to Maryland, where she worked as a reentry specialist for the Maryland Department of Public Safety and Correctional Services, a position from which she recently retired. It was her interview with the Bronx African American History Project, first published in the *Bronx County Historical Society Journal* in 2003, that launched the oral history phase of the BAAHP and persuaded many others to follow in her footsteps and put their stories on record.

Beatrice Bergland, who grew up in two Bronx neighborhoods where her experiences with race were strikingly different, has had a long career as a civil servant and religious leader. After graduation from high school, she went on to pursue a career in corrections and prison work, retiring as a lieutenant in the New York State Department of Corrections. Following her retirement, she devoted herself to work as a deacon in the Community Church of Morrisania, where she helped create that church's Black History Museum and its pioneering partnership with a church in Africa, an initiative that coincided with the rapid growth of African immigration to the Bronx.

Jacqueline (Jackie) Smith Bonneau grew up on Lyman Place in the South Bronx, the beneficiary of regular visits from her uncle, the legendary jazz pianist Thelonious Monk, and jam sessions at the apartment of Elmo Hope, who lived on the same block. Inspired by her uncle Thelonious, who lived with her family for two years after his Manhattan apartment suffered a fire and who named his song "Jackie-ing" for her, she became a pianist, composer, and educator. In recent years, she has concentrated on composing for and leading church choirs in Brooklyn, where she currently resides.

Arthur Crier, who passed away in 2004, was one of the Bronx's greatest doo-wop singers; a member of two urban harmonic groups based in his home neighborhood of Morrisania, the Halos and the Mellows; a background vocalist for some of the greatest rock-and-roll singers of his era, including Gene Pitney, Ben E. King, Dion, and the Coasters; and the lead artist on a Halos song, "Nag," which became a national hit. A brilliant songwriter and producer as well as singer, Arthur Crier worked for Motown Records from 1968 to 1972, where he had a chance to work with artists including the Temptations and Thelma Houston. Upon his return to the Bronx, Crier immersed himself in youth recreation as well as music, organizing teenage sports leagues along with talent shows at local housing projects, where the legendary Bronx hip-hop group the Cold Crush Brothers performed. Crier also helped produce many doo-wop reunion shows in the Bronx and elsewhere and helped launch his son Keith's vocal group, GQ, whose most popular hit was "Disco Nights."

Howie Evans, who grew up in the Morrisania section of the Bronx and graduated from Morris High School, is one of the nation's most distinguished sports journalists and a tireless advocate for black coaches, athletes, and communities. A graduate of the University of Maryland Eastern Shore, where he was a star point guard, Howie Evans began a career that included youth work in the New York City public schools, college coaching (at Fordham University and the University of Maryland Eastern Shore), and print and broadcast journalism. As senior sports editor for the *New York Amsterdam News*, a position he has held for more than forty years, Howie Evans has highlighted the accomplishments of black sports figures, exposed longstanding inequities at all levels of American sports, and championed youth recreation as a basic human right. In recognition of his efforts, he was selected as chairman of the New York Basketball

Hall of Fame, a position he still holds. He is widely regarded as the dean of American black sports journalism.

"Professor" Hetty Fox is a legendary South Bronx educator, musician, and community activist who is credited with saving her block—Lyman Place—from the fires that were sweeping the Morrisania neighborhood in the 1970s. The child of Guyanese immigrants, Hetty Fox was a star athlete and star student at St. Anthony of Padua Elementary School, winning the foul-shooting contest for Catholic girls' high schools in New York City. After graduating from Cathedral High School and Hunter College, she moved to California in the late 1960s, where she honed her performing skills in dance and African drumming while earning a master's degree and teaching sociology at California State College at Northridge. When she returned to the Bronx in 1970 to visit her family, Hetty Fox was terrified by the devastation striking her neighborhood and decided to devote herself to restoring a number of the buildings on her block. She turned two houses into community centers for children in the neighborhood, teaching them crafts and African languages; organized a play street for children during the summer; and did everything possible to keep other buildings on Lyman Place from burning. Today, forty-five years later, Hetty Fox still runs her play street, has holiday parties for youth, hosts visitors from around the world, and continues to fight for her block to be a place where it is safe for children to thrive and grow.

Avis Hanson, who passed away in 2015, was a teacher all her life, part of the first migration of black families from Harlem to the Morrisania section of the Bronx during the early years of the Depression. A top student in every school she attended, from elementary school through college, she began her teaching career at Morris High School, where in addition to teaching English she was the faculty advisor to the student newspaper. Among her students at Morris were Dr. Clara Rodriguez, a professor of sociology at Fordham University and a pioneering scholar in the field of Latino studies; and Dr. Robert Robinson, a scholar at the Center for Disease Control who specialized in tobacco addiction in the African American community. She then moved on to become chair of the English department at Taft High School in the West Bronx, and she concluded her distinguished career as a supervisor of all nonvocational subjects at Fashion Trades High School in Manhattan. Passionately devoted to her students, for whom she set the highest standards, Avis Hanson helped many young people navigate the kind of poverty and hardship she experienced in her own childhood, inspiring them to achieve both academic and professional success.

Dr. Vincent Harding, who passed away in 2014, was one of the nation's most distinguished historians, theologians, and civil rights leaders. Raised in the Bronx, Vincent Harding graduated from Morris High School in 1948 as class valedictorian and went on to earn his undergraduate degree at City College of New York and his doctorate in history from the University of Chicago. After becoming an ordained minister in the Mennonite Church, Dr. Harding relocated to Atlanta, where he became a close associate of Dr. Martin Luther King Jr., joining him in civil rights campaigns in Albany, Georgia, and Birmingham, Georgia, and helping him draft his famous 1967 speech opposing the Vietnam War. In the late 1960s, Dr. Harding became a pioneering figure in the Black Studies movement, helping found the Institute for the Black World, serving as a senior advisor to the acclaimed television series *Eyes on the Prize*, and writing several important books, including the acclaimed *There Is a River: The Black Freedom Struggle in America* and *Hope and History*. Dr. Harding and his wife Rosemarie remained active in social justice work until their passing, founding the Veterans of Hope Project at the Illiff School of Theology in Colorado, to encourage an intergenerational approach to social activism and spiritual renewal. The oral history with Dr. Harding that appears in this book was conducted at Morris High School, where Dr. Harding spoke eloquently of how the school, its principal, and his teachers helped shape his life and career.

Paul Himmelstein was a white Jewish resident of a nearly all-black block, Jennings Street in Morrisania, which was famous for producing doo-wop singers. Paul achieved local fame as a young singer in the mid-1950s. He began performing at local talent shows with his group, Paul Himmelstein and the Heartbreakers. They went on to perform at the Apollo, where the group won Amateur Night four weeks in a row. Offered a record contract as a solo artist, Paul refused. He dropped out of school and went through a long period of hard times, which included bouts of homelessness. After pulling his life together, Paul joined Local 32-B and found stable employment as a building service worker in Upper East Side apartment buildings. Spoken about with great fondness by many who grew up in Morrisania, Paul often returns to the neighborhood for the Old Timers' Day celebrations, which take place on the first Sunday of every August in Crotona Park.

Daphne Moss, who grew up on a predominantly Latino block in the Hunts Point section of the Bronx, has had an extraordinary career as a health professional, health educator, and school administrator. Following her graduation from Morris High School, she attended Bellevue School of Nursing and went on to spend ten years working as a registered nurse in venues ranging from recovery rooms to substance abuse programs. After earning an undergraduate degree from Fordham University Lincoln Center, she moved into the New York City public school system, first as a nurse in an elementary school in the Bronx, then as a teacher of nursing at the high school level. At Evander Childs High School in the North Bronx, where she began as a teacher, Daphne Moss Johnson became coordinator of the Health Careers Program while obtaining a master's degree from Lehman College. When the Evander program closed, she moved on to the School of Cooperative Technical Education in Manhattan, where she started a health careers program. She ultimately ended up as assistant principal of the school. After retiring from the NYC Department of Education, she continued to work in GED and technical training programs for adults. She has also appeared in several print and broadcast stories about her niece Kerry Washington, a nationally known film and television star, who once referred to her aunt on Twitter as "her favorite teacher."

Eugene "Gene" Norman, a lifelong Bronx resident, has had a distinguished career as an architect and public servant. Brought up on Kelly Street in the Hunts Point section of the Bronx, where General Colin Powell was a childhood friend, Gene graduated from Hunter College before pursuing architectural studies at Pratt Institute. First going into private practice, then joining the New York State Urban Development Corporation in 1972, Gene Norman worked on projects ranging from airports, to university campuses, to large-scale housing developments. In the mid-1970s, he began working with the Harlem Urban Development Corporation, where he eventually ascended to the position of executive vice president. In 1983, Gene Norman was appointed chairman of the Landmarks Preservation Commission of New York City, a position he held until 1989. Gene is currently helping spearhead *Save Harlem Now!,* a new preservation advocacy group. He remains a proud Bronx resident.

Joe Orange was born and raised in the Morrisania section of the Bronx and attended P.S. 99, J.H.S. 40, and Morris High School. Upon entering the seventh grade in J.H.S. 40, Joe was given a musical aptitude test and based on the results was placed in a special music class where, given a choice of instruments to play, he selected the trombone. The sound of the trombone was not foreign to Joe because his uncle, J. C. Higginbotham, who was considered the premier jazz trombonist in the world in the 1940s and 1950s, often stayed with Joe's family when he visited New York. Musically, Joe was also inspired by his cousin, Irene Higginbotham, a prolific songwriter who wrote (among many other songs) the classic jazz standard "Good Morning Heartache" for the jazz legend Billie Holiday. While a senior at Morris High School, Joe auditioned for and was selected to join the Newport Youth Band, led by the musician and educator Marshall Brown, one of eighteen people chosen out of the more than one thousand who applied. Performing with the Newport Youth Band put the finishing touches on Joe Orange's musical training, and following his graduation from high school he began his career as a professional musician by joining the pianist Eddie Palmieri's La Perfecta band. While with Eddie Palmieri's band on a full-time basis, Joe also freelanced and recorded with many other Latin bands, including Tito Puente, Mon Rivera, Larry Harlow, and Bobby Valentin. His musical career also includes full-time tenures with Lionel Hampton, Lloyd Price, Charlie Palmieri, Archie Shepp, and Herbie Mann. In the early 1960s, Joe left the music business to attend college full time and to launch a business career with a speciality in health administration. In this capacity he served as senior director of corporate accounts for Blue Cross Blue Shield of Greater New York, as executive director of customer relations for the Blue Cross Blue Shield Association, and as vice president of marketing and sales for Blue Cross Blue Shield of Maryland. Following his retirement, he has devoted himself to scholarship and charitable work, recieving a degree in ethnomusicology from Goddard College, helping fundraise and coordinate interviews for the Bronx African American History Project, and working with at-risk youth in his home community of Columbia, Maryland. He has two daughters, Karim, a celebrity makeup artist, and Kira, a nationally renowned educator who has been praised for contributing to the revival of public education in New Orleans following Hurricane Katrina.

Taur Orange, who grew up in the Bronxdale Houses, where Supreme Court Justice Sonya Sotomayor also lived, has had a distinguished career as an educator and advocate for marginalized students. Receiving her bachelor's degree in psychology from Wesleyan University and her master's degree in human relations from the New York Institute of Technology, she has served as director of opportunity programs at the Fashion Institute of Technology for the past twenty-five years, where she has mentored and guided thousands of students. Her passion for students was recently the subject of a story in *Humans of New York* that received more than three hundred thousand views. Along with teaching classes and counseling students at FIT, Taur Orange also serves as an interviewer and recruiter for Wesleyan University, where her efforts have contributed to that university's efforts to achieve class and race diversity. Her tireless efforts to motivate and inspire students have made her immensely popular at both institutions.

Jimmy Owens, a jazz trumpeter, composer, bandleader, and educator who learned to play trumpet in Bronx public schools, is one of the greatest musicians ever to come out of the Bronx. A National Endowment of the Arts Jazz Master and professor in the jazz studies program at the New School, Jimmy has performed with some of the greatest jazz musicians of the last fifty years and has traveled the world practicing his art. His career is a tribute to the remarkable musical culture of the Morrisania community where he grew up. He learned to play trumpet in J.H.S. 40's music and art program. Jimmy took trumpet lessons from the jazz trumpeter Donald Byrd and performed with the legendary jazz pianist Thelonious Monk (both Byrd and Monk lived in Morrisania in the 1960s). He was showcased at St. Augustine's Presbyterian Church while still a student at the High School of Music and Art and, with Joe Orange, was a member of the Newport Jazz Festival Youth Band. Jimmy, who lives abroad half the year and works with musicians around the world, has always treasured his Bronx roots. He wrote and performed his brilliant *Bronx Suite* for the tenth-anniversary celebration of the Bronx African History Project and played trumpet solos at the ceremonies co-naming two New York streets for two legendary South Bronx jazz musicians, Maxine Sullivan and Henry "Red" Allen.

Dr. Henry Pruitt is one of five siblings from the amazing Pruitt family of East 168th Street in Morrisania who became professional educators. The recipient of many advanced degrees, including a master's in science education from New York University and a doctorate from Columbia Teachers College, Henry Pruitt began his career in K–12 education in New York City, where he was an assistant headmaster at Harlem Prep before taking positions first as a teacher, then as an assistant principal, at J.H.S. 139. Upon moving to New Jersey, he became a middle school principal in Englewood, New Jersey, a trustee of William Patterson College, a member of the local school board in Teaneck, New Jersey, and the interim principal of a charter school in Plainfield, New Jersey. The recipient of many honors and awards, Henry Pruitt has also held positions in higher education, ranging from a graduate assistantship at Columbia Teachers College to positions as an assistant professor and department chair at Manhattan Community College. He was recently elected to the town council in Teaneck, New Jersey.

James "Jim" Pruitt, a beloved educator who spent his entire teaching career in the Bronx, is the youngest of five children of the amazing Pruitt family of East 168th Street. He is also a historian and community activist who is deeply involved in his church and in one of the organizations that helped shape his childhood, Camp Minisink. James Pruitt's career as a social studies teacher began at the school he graduated from, Morris High School. In 1969, he moved to a position as the director of the newly formed Upward Bound program at Fordham University, where one of his students was the famed singer Luther Vandross. In the ten years he ran that program, James Pruitt developed a powerful relationship with the young men he taught and mentored there, many of whom still get together for reunions under his direction. After leaving Fordham, he took a position as a social studies teacher and chair at John F. Kennedy High School in the Northwest Bronx. His retirement party from that school was attended by hundreds of people.

Andrea Ramsey is a lifelong Bronx resident. She attended P.S. 23, in the Morrisania Section in the Bronx, then Olinville J.H.S. and Evander Childs High School. After graduation she attended the Fashion Institute of Technology, majoring in textile design, and in 1961 she received an associate's degree and began work in the textile industry as a colorist. After raising her family, she returned to Fordham University and earned her bachelor's degree in fine arts in 1984, then went on to New York University to earn a master's degree in art therapy, in 1992. Andrea worked in the field of art therapy for twenty-one years, at Bellevue Hospital and North Central Bronx Hospital. She retired in 2009. She has volunteered at the New York Foundling Hospital and with Big Brothers & Big Sisters. She currently volunteers at the Bronx Woodlawn Cemetery and the WCS Bronx Zoo. Andrea loves spending time with family, traveling, painting, and writing. She is an avid historian and genealogist and is the vice president of the Jean Sampson Scott Greater NY Chapter of the Afro-American Historical and Genealogical Society. As a historian and genealogist, she is deeply aware of the importance of documenting the rich history of the Bronx.